C000108976

Saving for Retirement and Investing for Growth

REPORT OF THE CEPS-ECMI TASK FORCE ON LONG-TERM INVESTING AND RETIREMENT SAVINGS

CHAIR   **ALLAN POLACK**
CEO, Nordea Asset Management

RAPPORTEURS   **MIRZHA DE MANUEL ARAMENDÍA**
Research Fellow

KAREL LANNOO
Senior Research Fellow

CENTRE FOR EUROPEAN POLICY STUDIES
EUROPEAN CAPITAL MARKETS INSTITUTE
BRUSSELS

Disclaimer

This report is based on the discussions in the CEPS-ECMI Task Force on Long-Term Investing and Retirement Savings, which met on four separate occasions in 2012 and 2013. The policy recommendations offered at the beginning of this report reflect a general consensus reached by Task Force members, although not every member agrees with every aspect of each recommendation. A list of members, observers and invited guests of the Task Force can be found in Annex 2. The members were given the opportunity to comment on the draft final report, but its contents may only be attributed to the rapporteurs.

CEPS and ECMI gratefully acknowledge the financial support received for this Task Force from its members and the kind sponsoring by Carmignac Gestion.

The author, Mirzha de Manuel Aramendía, warmly thanks Karel Lannoo in his role of co-rapporteur; Allan Polack, Chairman of the Task Force, for his commitment to this project, impulse and guidance; Ole Stæhr for his important cooperation; Task Force members for their active participation and insightful comments; the European Commission, EIOPA and the OECD for their useful involvement as observers; Anne Harrington for her careful editing and advice; and CEPS staff for all their encouragement. Any errors or omissions are the sole responsibility of the author.

ISBN 978-94-6138-346-4
© Copyright 2013, CEPS and ECMI

All rights reserved. No part of this publication may be reproduced, stored in a retrieval system or transmitted in any form or by any means – electronic, mechanical, photocopying, recording or otherwise – without the prior permission of the Centre for European Policy Studies and the European Capital Markets Institute.

Centre for European Policy Studies
European Capital Markets Institute
Place du Congrès 1, B-1000 Brussels
Tel: (32.2) 229.39.11 | Fax: (32.2) 219.41.51
www.ceps.eu | www.eurocapitalmarkets.org

CONTENTS

List of Tables

List of Figures

List of Boxes

PREFACE

It is my pleasure to introduce this ambitious and forward-looking report of the CEPS-ECMI Task Force on Supporting Long-Term Investing and Retirement Savings. The report emphasises the potential of mobilising financial wealth for long-term investing to the benefit of both the citizens of Europe and the European economy.

When the words "long-term" are used, they may sound as if the matter were not urgent. Nothing, however, could be further from the truth, for Europe is facing a double challenge: a significant need for long-term investments – crucial levers for job creation, competitiveness and sustainable growth – and a growing pension gap, both of which call for resolute action.

A more prudent regulation in Europe following the 2008 economic and financial crisis has meant less availability of capital with the profile of being long-term and willing to accept risk. Capital markets are called to play an increasingly important role to channel savings into the productive economy.

Long-term capital is needed to fuel the competitive position of Europe in today's globalised world and protect the welfare of its citizens. It is of paramount importance that available patient capital can find its way into investment opportunities that push Europe's competiveness forward – whether fully private or in the form of public-private partnerships.

In parallel, the pension gap is widening and thus threatening the well-being of younger generations. In parts of Europe, a sustainable pension structure does either not exist or it is underfunded. Moreover, in countries where a pension structure does exist, many of the schemes are based on guaranteed structures or defined benefits. The low interest rates are challenging these models, dating back to periods with much higher interest rates and a more relaxed mechanism regarding mutual reallocation of wealth between beneficiaries. When combined with the demographic changes, we can expect a clash between generations where the future workforce will have to pay a substantial part of their income to support future pensioners. Apart from the moral aspect, it will dramatically dampen growth and lead to brain drain both at national and European level. Equally scary, and just as unacceptable, is the increasing risk of creating an impoverished class of the elderly in Europe.

Europe has not succeeded so far in building a single market for private pensions, where savings and related services can move freely across borders. Some member states have fairly solid systems, frequently occupational. But others lack even a basic framework. A well-articulated single market, however, could benefit both by delivering significant efficiencies. Lower costs, due to scale, are probably the most straightforward benefit, but a single market could also be made to deliver eased access and transferability.

In reforming the prudential rules for insurers and pension funds, via Solvency II and IORP II, respectively, it is possible to combine prudent governance with a higher traction for real assets. Governments do not deliver real returns. Only companies and businesses can do that. No sustainable retirement plans can be based primarily on investments in government bonds. By its very nature this would be degenerating for Europe. The increased prudency in the new regulation is needed, but with a few amendments the risk models could better reflect the long-term nature of pension and insurance plans.

This Task Force has focused on producing concrete proposals to address these challenges. The current and projected economic situation in Europe renders action urgent. It is unrealistic to wait for occupational pensions to develop in countries, industries or areas where no schemes exist today. Instead, our efforts should concentrate on personal pensions, in which employers may choose to contribute, and in gearing such pension solutions towards the long-term.

It has been a pleasure chairing this CEPS-ECMI Task Force, which brought together nearly 45 participants from industry, academia and policy-making. Despite the diverse interests around the table, I feel we managed to keep the focus on Europe and its citizens throughout the discussions. I would like to thank all contributors for their dedicated work.

I am also grateful to CEPS and ECMI for proposing and developing this Task Force. Hard work and enthusiasm were shown by Karel Lannoo, CEO of CEPS, and Mirzha de Manuel, author of the report. I would like to express my deepest respect to them for their work and commitment to this project.

Allan Polack
Chairman of the Task Force
CEO, Nordea Asset Management

EXECUTIVE SUMMARY AND POLICY RECOMMENDATIONS

Fostering long-term investing practices in funded pension plans, as well as retail access to these and other long-term investing solutions, probably constitutes the most significant opportunity to increase the availability of long-term financing in the European economy, while raising income adequacy at retirement. Europe faces a dual challenge: delivering strong and sustainable economic growth while bridging the widening pension gap, bringing strain on living standards and public finances. To realise these goals, the development of more inclusive, efficient and resilient retail investment markets plays a central role. Against this background, and based on the key conclusions summarised below, the members of this *CEPS ECMI Task Force* present the following recommendations to policy-makers and regulators.[1]

* * * * *

1. Place households, as end investors and beneficiaries, at the heart of the debate on long-term investing.

 ▶ Households are direct owners or indirect beneficiaries of 60% of financial assets in Europe. And they face a growing need to save more, and more efficiently, for retirement and other future consumption needs, implying long-term investment horizons, amidst growing longevity.

 ▶ At the macroeconomic level, long-term investing drives the productive capacity of an economy. But from a microeconomic perspective, it hangs on mobilising available long-term savings through investment solutions devised to maximise returns over the long-term, removing market and regulatory barriers.

> *Long-term investing by, or on behalf of, households.* Whether market or other risks are internalised by the intermediary – providing an insurance or a guarantee – or are borne directly by the beneficiaries, both solutions are compatible with long-term investing. By offering a guarantee the provider

---

[1] A full list of members (and observers) is presented in Annex 2. Please note the disclaimer featured in the copyright page of this report.

has a controlling incentive to realise long-term investing practices, albeit skewing asset allocation towards less-risky assets (bonds). In the absence of guarantees, more freedom in asset allocation represents a higher long-term investing potential but demands careful alignment of incentives and solution design. Pure long-term investing needs full illiquidity towards end investors during its life-cycle, eliminating the possibility of early redemptions. Yet, liquidity facilitates investor entry, competition and portability in fragmented markets.

Read more in Chapter 1 (Sections 2 and 3)

2. Enable and foster the access to long-term investing solutions for retail clients, including for retirement planning purposes.

▶ Retail investors and beneficiaries need easily accessible, high-quality and cost-efficient long-term savings and investment solutions. While such solutions exist in some member states, they are lacking or sub-standard in others.

▶ Standardisation of «default» solutions would help retail access by raising visibility, mitigating complexity and the burden of choice, and focusing competition on quality and costs. Such regulated solutions could hence be sold on an execution-only basis (see below).

▶ Any reform efforts should be mindful that financial exclusion in the markets for long-term savings/investments is widespread and only partially explained by disposable income. Broadly accessible solutions are needed, including for the most vulnerable.

Less-liquid investment funds for retail investors. EU product rules for retail balanced funds, with an asset allocation geared towards the long-term and limited redemption opportunities, would broaden access by retail investors to less-liquid assets. Such long-term balanced funds would complete the retail market, in addition to UCITS and the closed-end ELTIFs. Task Force members believe that the proposed closed-end ELTIFs would only be suitable for a minority of retail investors – given the high allocations to less-liquid assets – whilst long-term balanced funds could contribute significantly to financial inclusion. This Report weighs the merits of such balanced funds and explores an accompanying market structure.

Read more in Chapter 2 (Section 1)

3. Set a regulatory and supervisory framework strengthening the quality of long-term investment and retirement solutions – in a competitive market setting, delivering value primarily to investors.

▶ Investors in some markets perceive that funded pensions fail to deliver value. While volatile underlying market returns over the last years are primarily to blame, poor solution design and poorly organised markets for funded pensions also sometimes explain poor net performance.

▶ In addition to solution design, policy-makers should consider measures addressing market structure. The single market potential should be fully exploited in this respect – overcoming barriers such as the fragmentation of processing and inconsistent taxation principles.

Pan-European personal pensions. The provision of pensions is moving from traditional defined benefit to hybrid and defined contribution arrangements. Europe needs to equip itself better for this transition. An EU framework for personal pensions is needed to raise the quality of these solutions, notably by aligning incentives with long-term investing and retirement objectives while requiring appropriate risk management. An EU framework is also needed to address sub-optimal market structure and industrial organisation, including by widening accessibility and exploiting the potential of market integration. This Report considers key trade-offs in the design and delivery of personal pensions and suggests a blueprint for pan-European solutions, composed of six building blocks, with a clear retirement and long-term investing focus.

Read more in Chapter 3 and Table 10

4. Strengthen the framework for investor protection, while optimising it to promote long-term investing.

▶ When investing long-term, agency conflicts are magnified, as well as the cumulative impact of costs, given compounding. Investors may also be unfamiliar with long-term investment practices or limits on redemptions. Information and sale requirements should be attentive to these respects.

▶ While financial advice can help individuals make well-informed choices, the embedded costs ultimately reduce net returns and act as a barrier for small investors to enter the market. Actions to both moderate complexity and guide choices are needed to facilitate access to long-term investment and retirement solutions.

«Default solutions», advice and sale process. For retirement solutions, given their relevance for the income security of individuals and the cumulative

impact of costs on end benefits, any assessment of suitability should be based on broad market coverage and take full account of charges and costs. In a related vein, the large share of individuals who can hardly afford investment advice should be given the option to access cost-effective and high-quality «default solutions» on an execution-only basis. The words «default solutions» refer here to standardised solutions subject to product rules and available for purchase on an execution-only basis or within a pension plan, as described in this Report.

Read more in Chapter 2 (Section 3) and Chapter 3 (Section 4)

5. Continue to modernise the prudential rules and supervisory framework for the provision of guarantees.

▶ Task Force members recognise the merits of the Solvency II process and its role in driving greater sophistication in investment practices and risk management. Solvency II is also an important tool to safeguard financial stability and competition dynamics.

▶ It is crucial, however, that Solvency II reflects the risks effectively born in life insurance, including the mitigation effects derived from asset liability management (ALM). The 'matching adjustment' is central in this respect but the effects of ALM should also be recognised in capital charges.

▶ Task Force members support the approximation of qualitative aspects in national IORP legislation. As for quantitative aspects, more research is needed, given the diversity of the sector in Europe, including in terms of security and adjustment mechanisms. Yet, arbitrage between insurer and pension fund operations, where comparable, should be avoided.

Long-term investing within Solvency II. Reflecting the fundamentals of asset liability management is important for capturing the risks to which insurers and beneficiaries are actually exposed. It is essential to support best practices in the operation of life insurance and accurate reporting to stakeholders. In addition, extending the eligibility for the 'matching adjustment' to securities with an expected cash-flow profile similar to bonds could facilitate long-term investing, including in infrastructure and others. Moreover, capital charges for sovereign debt should be reconciled with economic reality to avoid distorting asset allocation to the detriment of long-term investing. This Report considers long-term investing when guarantees are offered and necessitate prudential requirements.

Read more in Chapter 1 (Section 3)

The reform of the IORP directive. The diversity of occupational pensions in Europe calls for caution on the approximation of prudential rules. The reform of the IORP directive should distinguish between dealing with legacy issues versus prospectively devising a framework for the future workplace pensions in Europe. Quantitative requirements should fully reflect the characteristics of pension contracts and the distribution of risks among participants, sponsor and any other stakeholder. Ultimately, given the magnitude of pension funds as operators in financial markets and the need to preserve financial stability, quantitative requirements should be approximated – taking due account of the diversity of pension funds and national pension systems. Approximation should not be undertaken in haste and member states should retain flexibility to deal with instances of underfunding.

Read more in Chapter 2 (Section 2)

* * * * *

In sum, the Task Force members believe the recommendations above would contribute to the development of more inclusive, efficient and resilient retail investment markets, which are better equipped and more committed to deliver value over the long-term for beneficiaries. In so doing, they believe long-term investing could be significantly increased, to the benefit of both investors and the economy. In addition to high quality intermediated solutions for long-term investing, Task Force members also encourage the development of accessible markets for retail direct investments in equities and, specially, bonds – as an additional way to foster long-term investing and capital markets in Europe. Collective investment schemes offer however better diversification than direct access by retail investors.

* * * * *

1. SETTING THE SCENE: LONG-TERM INVESTING AND RETIREMENT SAVINGS IN EUROPE

This first chapter provides an overview of the multifaceted concept of long-term investing and a stylised picture of both retail and institutional investing today, setting the scene for the remaining two chapters of the report. It explains the focus of the Task Force in enabling and promoting long-term investing in the interest of beneficiaries.

Beyond the precise definition of long-term investing from a macroeconomic perspective, this chapter argues that in practical terms what matters is the implementation of long-term investing through product mix and business model innovation, as well as market settings and structures, in order to stimulate supply and satisfy unmet demand for long-term investing among investors and beneficiaries.

1.1 What is long-term investing?

Long-term investing is a multi-faceted concept...

In defining long-term investing, the focus can be placed on different elements: investors themselves, investment strategies and behaviour, asset classes or even the ultimate non-financial underlying. It is also possible to follow a macro or a micro approach to the definition of long-term investing. Definitions can be based on objective factors (for instance investment horizons) or more subjective considerations, such as social usefulness.

➤ *The identification of long-term investors*

Long-term investing has been frequently defined with reference to the role of **institutional investors** as providers of patient, engaged and productive capital (OECD, 2013a). This includes notably defined benefit pension funds and life insurers – with an average duration of their liabilities of 7 to 15 years and assets under management in excess of $22 trillion globally – but also family offices, endowments and foundations, and sovereign wealth funds – with longer liability profiles but global assets below $6 trillion (World Economic Forum & Oliver Wyman, 2011).

A long-term investor depends chiefly on its liability profile and its ability to ride out short-term volatility while taking advantage of low prices and illiquid investment opportunities. A long-term investor therefore has no specific short-term liabilities or liquidity demands, or otherwise these are small in proportion to its total portfolio (Ang & Kjaer, 2011).

Institutional investors are widely recognised as "the natural providers of long-term finance in the financial system" (FSB, 2013) to the extent that the duration of their liabilities is suited to fund assets with long lifecycles.[2] Hence, the question is not whether institutional investors can perform long-term investing but the extent to which they do and whether any market or regulatory barriers distort their behaviour.[3]

Other institutions also perform a role as long-term investors despite having a liability profile that may be shorter-term or more uncertain than the ones above. **Banks** are the most important long-term investors by size in many jurisdictions. In Europe, they provide over 50% of long-term investing, and in China over 70% while in the US less than 20% (G30, 2013, p. 29). More than half of the long-term lending by banks are mortgages, however, which frequently finance the consumption of housing rather than "the expansion of productive capacity in the economy"(G30, 2013, p. 30).

The future contribution of banks to long-term investing is uncertain, as they undergo a process of deleveraging and adjustment following the 2008 financial crisis and the introduction of new regulations under Basel III. From a financial stability perspective, reduced incentives for banks to fund long-term investments on short-term liabilities are welcomed (FSB, 2013, p. 14), but they open a transition period where it is crucial to i) maximise the long-term potential of institutional investors and ii) promote the development of market-based finance, particularly in Europe.

The role of banks, **capital markets** and institutional investors should not be considered in isolation, however. Structured finance can help channel long-term funding towards long-term investment opportunities via capital markets, allowing institutional investors and beneficiaries to profit from the underwriting expertise of local bank branches. High-quality securitisation can

---

[2] Only fixed and long-term liabilities allow institutional investors to access less-liquid asset classes, without jeopardising financial stability derived from potential liquidity shortfalls or maturity mismatches.

[3] Such is the focus of the OECD project on 'institutional investors and long-term investing', in addition to the promotion of responsible share ownership (OECD, 2013). A private initiative, the Long-term Investors Club, also aims at clarifying the status of long-term investors, with respect to accounting and prudential rules, and promoting long-term investing. Section 1.4 considers institutional long-term investment today.

indeed be useful in this respect. The challenge is to control some of the risks inherent in the process, such as complexity, transparency and volume-based incentives, which led to the 2008 sub-prime crisis.[4]

Investment funds also play a useful role in long-term investing, depending on their investment objectives and redemption profile. Retail funds are considered institutional investors (OECD, 2013a). Traditional retail funds, such as UCITS (undertakings for collective investment in transferable securities) or mutual funds, offer high liquidity to investors, in terms of redemptions. Yet, their investment objectives may project over the long-term and their volume of assets under management may remain stable over time. Examples are 'buy and hold' strategies and some target-date funds. Other retail funds invest primarily or partially in less-liquid assets under redemption policies that incorporate restrictions, e.g. limited windows, advanced notice requirements and lock-in periods.

While identifying the long-term investors currently operating in the marketplace is certainly useful in order to promote their role, it should not obscure the potential for innovation in the business model and product mix, nor the fiduciary role of institutional investors.

➢ *Asset classes that are compatible or require long-term investing*

Most asset classes are not short-term or long-term per se but can be part of long-term investing depending both on the strategy of the investor and the ultimate non-financial underlying. As a general rule, asset classes that are less-liquid or have maturities that extend beyond the business cycle require long-term investing (FSB, 2013). The illiquidity elicits the commitment to the assets, which the investor is unlikely to be able to sell at short notice at fair value. It increases not only the likelihood of large costs in case of early exit but also results in very certain and palpable entry costs – including discovery, appraisal, valuation and legal costs – given the lack of public markets.

Asset classes compatible with long-term investing include fixed-income under long maturities (at least 10 years or in line with business cycle), listed equity, non-listed equity and infrastructure (WEF-OW, 2011). But a number of factors determine the extent to which the use of these instruments is longer-term:

○ Equity vs. fixed-income risk. The payoff and risk characteristics of long-term investments are more akin to equity than to debt. This is very much

---

[4] An industry initiative, Prime Collateralised Securities (PCS, 2013), was launched in 2012 to help revive the securitisation market in Europe, badly hit following the 2008 financial crisis. The initiative is aimed at promoting securitisation by issuing standards and awarding the PCS label based on criteria of quality, transparency, simplicity and standardisation.

the case in 'project finance' where the return on investment depends on the project cash flow rather than the financial strength of a counterparty (see below). In this context however, structured finance provides solutions to identify and disaggregate risks, allocating them to different investors in line with their position, capabilities and risk appetite (Yescombe, 2002).

○ Listed vs. non-listed equity. While all equity instruments confer similar rights onto shareholders, equities listed in public markets offer liquidity to investors. Non-listed equities therefore require a longer-term commitment from investors. At the same time, perceived pressure on quarterly earnings in public markets is inducing some healthy and mature listed companies to consider going private, as they feel public markets would not support any conversion producing results over the long-term rather than in the next few quarters.[5]

○ Tradable vs. held to maturity. Fixed-income assets purchased to be held to maturity provide a stable funding basis for issuers, helping to balance the pressure on short-term performance from public markets. From the point of view of the investor, holding a debt instrument to maturity results in a mutation of relevant risks; spread risk – the risk of losses given short-term market fluctuations in the valuation of an instrument – gives way to default risk – the risk that the issuer may default during the life of the instrument.

○ Direct vs. intermediated access. Additional intermediation or outsourcing allows institutional investors – asset owners in this context – to i) access expertise outside mainstream asset classes and ii) pool their capital with similar investors, where required by the sheer size of the investment or prudent to benefit from diversification. It does result however in agency conflicts and costs, given the difficulty in aligning the interests of intermediaries and asset owners.[6] Direct access is not always feasible but has the potential to optimise strategy and maximise returns net of fees. The extent to which institutional investors can perform direct access depends not only on the size of their balance sheet but also on their willingness to generate internal expertise and capabilities. Market size explains the average size of institutional investors and depends, in the EU context, on the level of integration of the single market.

---

[5] The European Commission proposed in 2011 to forego the regulatory requirement for quarterly reporting [COM (2011) 683 final].

[6] So far policy action to align interests has focused on remuneration and has affected more directly managers of investment funds (while for institutional investors, remuneration rules tend more to pursue a financial stability objective).

○ Strategic vs. satellite investing. For equity instruments, the difference is usually made between major stakes held for strategic purposes and other 'satellite' investments that help achieve diversification.[7] Strategic holdings are more likely to be held over the long-term and to command the interest of asset owners for active engagement. In effect, the benefits from active share ownership and engagement relate positively to the amount of capital committed and the investment horizon.

The figure below, adapted from the report of the World Economic Forum and Oliver Wyman (2011) on long-term investing, presents an overview of asset classes and their compatibility with long-term investing.

Figure 1. Liquidity, life-cycle and compatibility with long-term investing for selected asset classes

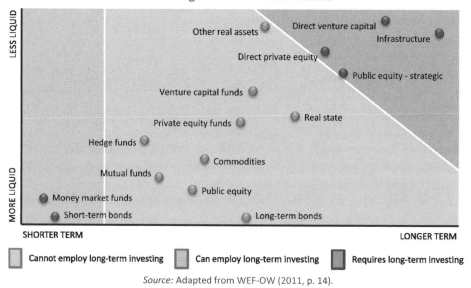

Source: Adapted from WEF-OW (2011, p. 14).

> *The ultimate non-financial underlying of long-term investing*

The Group of Thirty (2013), the European Commission (2013a) and the FSB (2013) all propose similar definitions of long-term investment based on the concept of gross fixed-capital formation in national accounting. Long-term investing would therefore include investment in infrastructure, new real estate development, equipment and software – *tangibles* – as well as in education,

---

[7] Even when asset allocation remains stable, however, an asset owner may change funds or mandates at short intervals, based on short-term performance, which is an issue of concern regarding long-term investing.

research and development – *intangibles*. It would exclude both financial capital formation (financing for consumption smoothing, financial institutions and liquidity or payments) and consumption, including consumer durables. The focus is hence on productive investment that can extend the frontiers of productivity, competitiveness and growth in an economy.

The European Commission further specifies the ultimate underlying of long-term investing in line with the priorities of its broader growth strategy[8]: i) energy, transport and communication infrastructures, ii) industrial and service facilities, iii) housing and iv) climate change and eco-innovation technologies.[9] The challenge of delimiting the scope of these different underlyings should not be underestimated, as highlighted for instance by the OECD (2011) with respect to infrastructure (Della Croce, 2011).

It is worth noting in addition that, given the underlyings identified, the notion of long-term investing appears closely connected to 'project finance', meaning the financing of projects where investors bear (and frequently manage to some extent) technical, environmental, economic and political risks specific to the project, and the return on their investment depends chiefly on the cash flow generated by the project rather than the financial standing of any counterparty (Yescombe, 2002). The pursuit of long-term investing practices should also be stimulated, however, in the field of traditional equities and bonds.

➤ *Long-term investment behaviour and incentives*

Long-term investing is also defined from a behavioural perspective, focusing on the intent of a qualified investor to hold an asset over an indefinite period of time (WEF-OW, 2011). The intent, expertise, expectations and ultimately the behaviour and incentives of the investor are indeed as important as its liability horizon.

Behaviour and incentives are discussed in this context both to explain the apparent short-term bias of some agents and prescribe solutions that would promote long-term investing. Within the asset management value chain, most stakeholders identify performance and risk measurement as the main hurdle for long-term investing:

---

[8] The Europe 2020 strategy (ec.europa.eu/europe2020) and the development of its 'flagship' initiatives, including in terms of industrial policy (EC, 2012), innovation policy (EC, 2010) and integrated European infrastructures (EC, 2011).

[9] These priorities also inform the request from the Commission (2012a) to EIOPA to calibrate capital charges for long-term investing within Solvency II. In addition, the financing of small- and medium-sized enterprises (SMEs), social business financing and socially responsible investments – as presented in EC (2011b) and EC (2013b) respectively – are also regarded as elements of long-term investing (EC, 2013a, p. 1 and p. 15).

○ Performance measurement in investment mandates is frequently based on a market benchmark, which the manager is called to outperform. The impact of benchmarks extends not only to the selection and appraisal of investment opportunities but also the remuneration of managers. Benchmarks that account for long-term investment horizons or the life-cycle of less-liquid asset classes are not readily available. Fundamental benchmarks, based on sector and macroeconomic conditions rather than market performance, can also play a role in disentangling individual from peer performance.

○ Typical risk measurement methodologies are based on past performance and short-term horizons, which result in short-term volatility weighing excessively in investment decisions. The impact of these methodologies on asset allocation and risk management is magnified by its use for compliance and regulatory purposes.[10] The perceived over-reliance on methodologies such as value-at-risk (VaR)[11] is controversial not only from the perspective of long-term investing but also due to the widespread belief that it contributed deeply to the irrational exuberance that led to the 2008 financial crisis (Turner, 2009; De Larosière et al., 2009).

From the perspective of behaviour and incentives, long-term investing can be defined as an investment process that takes due account of the potential and characteristics of longer-term holding periods and less-liquid asset classes. It involves notably the use of aligned performance and risk measurement tools. Examples are: i) establishing absolute return targets over relative performance, ii) considering cash-flows and underlying economic drivers over market prices, iii) monitoring indications of potential short-term bias, such as high turnover, iv) evaluating managers over extended periods of time and market circumstances and most importantly v) framing risk metrics within broader

---

[10] For instance, the SCR (solvency capital requirement) under Solvency II is base on a VaR measure calibrated to a 99.5% confidence level over a one-year time horizon (Art. 101) – which corresponds to the worst loss one could expect in any single year in the next 200 years, assuming normally distributed returns and based on historical market data. In CRD IV (Credit Requirements Directive) VaR is used for the purpose of calculating own funds (Art. 186). In UCITS, so-called 'global exposure' is limited with reference to VaR (ESMA guidelines, CESR/10-788).

[11] Value at risk (VaR) is an estimation of the maximum potential decrease in the market value of a portfolio based on historical market data and assuming a given distribution of returns (typically, the normal distribution) with a given confidence level. For instance, a VaR (20 days, 99%) of €5 million means that, under normally distributed returns in the marketplace, there is a 99% probability that a portfolio will not lose more than €5 million in value in 20 trading days. VaR does not provide information about potential loss outside the confidence interval.

analytical and operational frameworks, shifting the focus from measurement to management (WEF-OW, 2011; de Manuel & Lannoo, 2012, p. 77).

Active ownership (engagement) and the consideration of environmental, social and governance (ESG) factors are also an integral part of long-term investing, as they drive incentives in a direction that promotes voice over exit, longer holding periods and comprehensive risk management (Hirschman, 1970; IISD, 2012; IRI, 2006).

➢ *In sum...*

The concept of long-term investing is multi-faceted (Table 1 below summarises the definitions of long-term investing by key institutions). A long-term *investor* is defined chiefly by its liability profile and investment philosophy, while long-term *assets* are defined by their duration or life cycle, in practice linked to their non-financial underlying and its potential externalities. The goals pursued by policy action refer both to *financial stability* – setting the right incentives for long-term investments to be funded by long-term liabilities – and sustained *economic growth* – by removing artificial deterrents and promoting investment in infrastructure, equipment, education and research and development, while encouraging the consideration of ESG criteria and active ownership. The key question remains how to bring these goals forward in practice.

Table 1. Definitions of long-term investing provided by key institutions

Group of Thirty (2013)	*"Long-term financing* refers to the provision of long-dated funds to pay for capital-intensive undertakings that have multi-year payback periods. *Long-term investment* is spending on the tangible and intangible assets that can expand the productive capacity of an economy."
European Commission (2013)	*"Long-term investment* is the formation of long-lived capital, covering tangible assets and intangible assets that boost innovation and competitiveness."
OECD (2011)	*"Responsible and longer-term investment* among institutional investors shares the following features: more patient capital that acts in a counter-cyclical manner; ongoing and direct engagement as shareholders and consideration of environmental and other longer-term risks; and an active role in the financing of long-term, productive activities that support sustainable growth."
WEF - OW (2011)	*"Long-term investing* can be usefully defined as investing with the expectation of holding an asset for an indefinite period of time by an investor with the capability to do so."
Kay (2012)	Portrays a broad distinction between investing, focused on the activities of the company (business, strategy, profits) and trading, focused on the market for shares of a company (order flow, short-term correlations, arbitrage opportunities).

Source: As indicated, quotes shortened and rearranged by the author.

1.2   What is the focus of this report?

Beneficiaries should be brought to the discussion...

The section above explored the definition of long-term investing from various perspectives – referring to investors, asset classes, underlyings and behaviour – and presented the main approaches and policy priorities identified by the OECD, the Financial Stability Board (FSB) and the European Commission. Policy-makers have identified two key macro-goals: long-term financing and productive investments. To realise these goals however, our attention should focus on micro-questions and beneficiaries.

Households account directly for approximately 43% ($23 trillion) of financial assets owned by residents in Western Europe (McKinsey Global Institute, 2011). And they are the beneficiaries of a further $10 trillion held by institutional investors in pension funds, individual retirement accounts and life insurance, that is, an additional 18% to 20% of assets. The remainder is held by non-life insurers (10% or $5 trillion) and banks (22% or $12 trillion). In total therefore, households are the direct owners or indirect beneficiaries of at least 60% of financial assets in Europe (Figure 2). Section 1.3 and chapter 3 consider household wealth in more detail.

Figure 2. Financial assets owned by residents in Western Europe, 2010

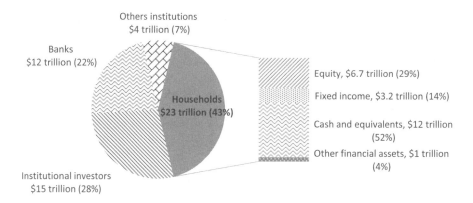

Note: Western Europe refers to EU-15, Switzerland and Norway. Institutional investors include pension funds, individual retirement accounts (IRAs), insurance undertakings, endowments and foundations. Other institutions refer to non-financial corporations, central banks and sovereign wealth funds. Equity includes listed equity shares and equities held via mutual funds.

Source: McKinsey Global Institute (2011).

Beyond the widespread acknowledgement that institutional investors are "the most natural providers of long-term finance in the financial system" (FSB, 2013), the debate on long-term investing would probably benefit from further reflection on the mobilisation of household wealth and the product offerings and business models of both insurance and asset management undertakings.

The relevance of households to long-term investing arises therefore both from i) being the largest owner and beneficiary of financial assets in Western Europe and globally, and ii) the long-term horizon inherent in saving and investing for major future consumption needs, including notably retirement. Current macroeconomic conditions, which project into the future, such as fiscal sustainability, low interest rates and ageing, are determining factors.

To date, the promotion of financial stability and sustainable economic growth have driven the debate on long-term investing. By contrast, the members of the CEPS-ECMI Task Force on Long-term Investing and Retirement Savings aimed to focus on the microeconomic level by bringing the interests of beneficiaries forward and discussing potential solutions for the share of their savings that could benefit from long-term investing.

Our focus is on retail investment products...

The potential of mobilising household financial wealth for long-term investing is elicited both by its size and the long-term horizons involved in investing for retirement. Against this background, the Task Force focused on the interest of beneficiaries to access long-term retail investment products.

Retail investment products allow individuals to accumulate savings and gain market exposure (investment funds), a guaranteed return (insurance policies) or a combination of both. Investment funds tend to offer investors high liquidity – the possibility to redeem daily – whereas insurance policies tend to incorporate limits to redemptions.

The redemption policy towards investors determines the level of certainty and extension of the liability profile of the originator, although total assets under management may remain stable within certain thresholds even in the presence of high liquidity for investors, particularly for funds offering competitive pricing and standardised diversification.

Products offering high liquidity can be utilised by retail investors for long-term investing purposes, for instance to invest in a diversified equity basket with the intent of holding that basket over an indefinite period of time. Under such an investment horizon, an investor may however also wish to invest in less-liquid assets, such as unlisted equity, real estate or infrastructure.

The liquidity of the underlying (the ability to sell it in the marketplace at short notice and fair value) and of the product units (the ability to redeem equally at short notice and fair value) are linked in several respects:

- ◦ From a financial stability perspective, the liquidity of units and underlying should be in line to mitigate the risk of destabilising fire-sales and failure to meet redemptions (de Manuel & Lannoo, 2012, p. 33). This principle holds whether market risks fall entirely on the investor or only partially – when a guarantee is given as to principal or return, the provider should in addition be duly capitalised.

○ From a retail investor perspective, the liquidity of product units is relevant in three respects: i) higher liquidity facilitates investor entry, since it lowers commitment and increases perceived empowerment; ii) enables competition for existing pools of savings, as well as portability in fragmented markets; but iii) may result in foregone returns, given the illiquidity premium, and lower diversification, as it inhibits access to less-liquid asset classes.[12]

○ From a long-term investing perspective, asset classes with longer maturities or less-liquidity are better funded by sources with similar features for investors. Similarly, longer liability profiles generally increase the incentives for responsible engagement.

Retail investment products offering lower liquidity therefore have the potential to offer higher returns and diversification to investors who are able to commit their capital over the long-term and willing to accept some limits to redemptions. However, since lower liquidity limits competition to administer existing pools of savings, the optimal level of liquidity towards investors also depends on market circumstances. For instance, in the European context, given incomplete integration of national markets, low liquidity could further limit cross-border flows and increase fragmentation. Similarly, lack of investor familiarity with illiquid products could lead to sub-optimal allocation. Liquidity, however, is a continuum that allows for intermediate solutions. Moreover, actions could also be undertaken to remove the ancillary barriers above – consolidating the single market, improving investor education or offering incentives to invest in less-liquid products.

In view of the former, the Task Force and this report focus on less-liquid retail investment products, defined by their i) *purpose* – serving retail investors to accumulate savings and gain market exposure in order to maintain or increase the inflation-adjusted value of those savings; ii) *investment horizon* – in excess of 10 years; iii) *packaging* – incorporating limits to redemptions that result in a certain liability profile for the originator and iv) *underlying* – which includes assets with long-term maturities and life cycles.

Section 1.3 considers long-term retail investing today in more detail, including the liquidity profile of available retail investment products.

---

[12] For a review of the academic literature referring to the illiquidity premium, refer to EDHEC-Risk (2010).

Including personal retirement schemes...

The accumulation and investment of retirement savings, undertaken from an early age, throughout working life and even during retirement, is probably the best example of the potential for long-term investing by individuals.

The provision of retirement income takes different forms across countries and even professions. Most pension systems are based on three tiers: i) government or social security benefits, ii) occupational schemes and iii) individual savings. The term 'personal pensions' is used to refer to private pension solutions to which the employer may or may not make contributions, and hence can be part of the last two tiers (chapter 3).

The importance of personal retirement schemes is elicited by demographic and economic trends. Longer life expectancies mean larger pools of capital will be needed to support income adequacy upon retirement.[13] While the inversion of the age pyramid – more people receiving benefits than financing them – puts a strain on government and social security benefits to meet the challenge on their own.[14] Personal pensions are therefore called upon to supplement income adequacy.

Supporting the development of personal pensions in order to foster adequacy is indeed among the priorities identified by the European Commission (2012c) in its agenda for adequate, safe and sustainable pensions.

The balance between safety and adequacy is hard to strike, however, notably in an environment of persistently low interest rates and dismal growth. Pension safety refers to the provision of guarantees, mostly supported by fixed-income strategies, devised to match assets and liabilities. But under low interest rates, providers are forced to re-orient their product offerings towards more limited, lower and conditional guarantees (lower adequacy and/or safety). Where no guarantees are offered, different investment strategies are possible, holding the potential for higher returns (potentially higher adequacy) but also higher risks (lower safety).

Long-term investing is in line with the interest of beneficiaries in both product categories. A long-term liability profile allows product providers to hold assets to maturity, riding-out short-term volatility and concentrating on the economic fundamentals of the underlying. It also allows them to invest in equity markets with a long-term focus, which they can steer through engagement. And finally,

---

[13] By 2060, life expectancy at birth is expected to raise by 7.9 years for men and 6.5 for women, compared to 2010 (European Commission, 2012b).

[14] By 2060, there will be two people of working age for every person over 65 – in 2010 there were four people (European Commission, 2010a).

they are able to invest in less-liquid assets and access the premia linked to their illiquidity.

To maximise long-term investing in personal pensions, there are nevertheless a number of barriers to overcome, including: i) the difficulty in separating short-term volatility from default risk, where assets are held to maturity; ii) cognitive limitations and behavioural biases, including myopic risk aversion, leading to sub-optimal decisions among retail investors; and iii) the structure of the market for personal pensions which may limit its ability to deliver full value to investors. Section 1.4 considers the first barrier, including the role of prudential rules, while chapters 2 and 3 consider the other two, with regard to investor protection and the markets for long-term investment solutions and pensions.

1.3   Retail long-term investing today

The previous section narrowed the focus of this report to the interest of retail investors and beneficiaries in accessing long-term investments, notably for the purpose of retirement provision. As noted above, households are direct owners or indirect beneficiaries of over 60% of financial assets in Europe and have high potential as long-term investors, given the horizons linked to saving for major future consumption needs, including retirement.

This section considers retail long-term investment, by referring to the diversity, degree of liquidity and intermediation of retail investments in Europe, and the related institutional setting.

A diverse picture in Europe...

The distribution of household financial wealth across financial instruments and solutions is not homogenous within the EU.[15] As shown in Figure 3, allocations to pension schemes and life insurance policies in some member states are large, both in absolute and relative terms, whereas in others, households allocate 20% or less of their financial wealth to retirement solutions. Among major economies, the Netherlands, UK and France are the best positioned, while Italy and Spain lag far behind.

This diversity is attributable to multiple reasons, such as: i) total wealth and the balance between consumption and savings; ii) the institutional setting for retirement provision and the strength of first-pillar pensions; iii) prevailing perceptions about retirement, the role of the state and expectations about

---

[15] There is no homogeneity either in the weight of non-financial wealth (land and dwellings) in total wealth or its distribution. For instance, according to OECD statistics for 2010, land accounted for 21% of total household wealth in the Netherlands, compared to 43% in France, and dwellings for 22% and 37%, respectively.

future income; iv) lay perceptions about financial instruments, risk aversion and investment horizons, v) the relative weight of non-financial assets and attitudes versus real estate,[16] vi) financial shrewdness and cost awareness and vii) taxation and other exogenous incentives.

Yet, despite this diversity, Europeans from all origins face a growing need to save more for retirement, which should increase allocations to targeted investment and insurance solutions, promoting convergence. Supporting the development of long-term savings is important, not only to enhance retirement incomes, but also to promote long-term investing and macroeconomic convergence within Europe (European Commission, 2013a, 2012c, 2012d).[17]

Figure 3. Distribution of European household financial holdings, end 2011 (€ billion)

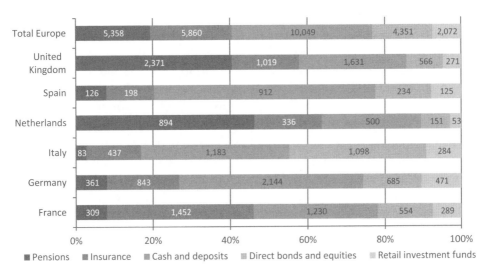

Note: Total Europe includes Austria, Belgium, Czech Republic, Denmark, Finland, France, Germany, Greece, Hungary, Ireland, Italy, the Netherlands, Norway, Poland, Portugal, Slovak Republic, Spain, Sweden, Switzerland and the UK. Insurance includes life and composite undertakings.

Source: Boston Consulting Group.

---

[16] Many Europeans save primarily by investing in real estate, including their own dwelling. Other Europeans prefer to rent their residence. The return on one's dwelling depends on the mix of purchase versus rent prices, financing conditions, taxation and the evolution of real estate prices.

[17] The development and promotion of complementary retirement savings is one of the recommendations issued by the European Commission to member states through the 'Annual Growth Surveys'. These surveys are one of the mechanisms to strengthen macroeconomic policy coordination in the EU (the 'European Semester' framework).

Intermediated over direct access...

About 45% of household financial assets in Europe are not held directly but via intermediaries. An additional 35% is held in cash or deposits, while only 20% is estimated to correspond to direct bond and equity holdings (Figure 4). Diversity is also present in this respect, with Italy boasting twice the European average in direct holdings, thanks to a competitive and accessible bond market for retail investors.

Intermediation allows investors to benefit from professional management and diversification. Within retirement solutions, intermediation is indispensable to arbitrate insurance, repartition and solidarity mechanisms. These advantages make intermediation central to long-term investing by households – although not all forms of intermediation are conducive to long-term investing as discussed in section 1.1.

Intermediation does however entail agency conflicts between the parties to the contractual relationship – household and provider – as their interests diverge. It also entails charges and costs, which depending on competition dynamics, can be sizeable and severely dampen net returns (EC, 2009). Investor protection and competition policies are hence important to ensure intermediation delivers value primarily to beneficiaries rather than providers.

When investing long-term, agency conflicts and the effects of charges and costs (given compounding) are magnified. While the interest of beneficiaries would be to maximise long-term performance, intermediaries may pay more attention to shorter-term results – given for instance reporting and valuation practices, market pressures or staff remuneration and tenures. Preserving the interest of beneficiaries may therefore warrant further public intervention in the markets for long-term and retirement savings (section 2.3, chapter 3 and Box 5).

Beyond intermediation, long-term investing by households may also take place via direct holdings of equity and bonds and other simple instruments. In fact, direct holdings by households may provide more patient capital (with lower turnover) than some forms of intermediation. Direct access by retail investors to some market segments, however, in particular for corporate and sovereign bonds, is limited in most member states, both with regard to national and EU issuance (see section 2.4).

Figure 4. Intermediation in European household financial holdings, end 2011 (€ trillion)

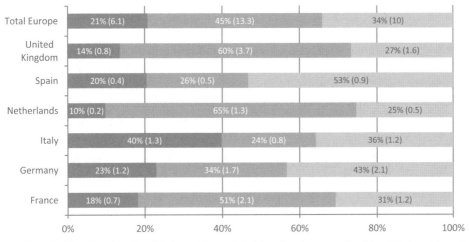

Direct holdings (bonds and equities) Intermediated (pension, insurance, funds) Cash and deposits

Note: Total Europe includes Austria, Belgium, Czech Republic, Denmark, Finland, France, Germany, Greece, Hungary, Ireland, Italy, the Netherlands, Norway, Poland, Portugal, Slovak Republic, Spain, Sweden, Switzerland and the UK. Insurance includes life and composite undertakings.

Source: Boston Consulting Group.

Liquid over illiquid products...

Over 90% of intermediated financial holdings by households are estimated to be moderately to fully illiquid, meaning they incorporate important restrictions on early redemptions or may only be redeemed upon maturity (typically upon retirement). This is the 40% of household financial wealth held in pensions and life insurance solutions.[18] A similar percentage is held in cash or bank deposits and money market funds (the most liquid end of the spectrum) while 22% is invested in bonds, equities and investment funds – mostly UCITS whose units or shares can be redeemed daily (Figure 5).

Illiquidity is linked to long-term investing to the extent that less-liquid asset classes typically require long-term funding. And long-term investing practices can only be safely pursued by intermediaries (on behalf of investors) if their liability profile is stable and can be anticipated with sufficient certainty – which involves restrictions on redemptions, either explicit or implicit in the event of market distress leading to mass redemptions. Life insurance and pension funds are positioned at the less-liquid end of the spectrum.

---

[18] Some pension solutions and life insurance policies are redeemable before retirement but entail fees or penalties (endogenous barriers). In addition, taxation arrangements also tend to deter early redemptions (exogenous barriers).

Diversity in the liquidity of holdings is observable not only at the macro but also at micro level. In absolute terms, the individual weight of deposits and pension funds/life insurance is similar in Europe (Figure 5). However, ECB (2013) data reveal that deposits are the most prevalent financial asset, owned by 96% of households, recording a median value (conditional on ownership) of €6,100. By way of contrast, voluntary private pensions and whole life insurance are held by only 33% of households at an average value of €11,900. It follows therefore that, despite similar weight in absolute terms, the distribution of deposits versus pension funds/life insurance is very unequal at the micro-level.

The question that is the most pertinent but probably also the most difficult to answer is the share of holdings in cash and deposits that are long-term and might find better returns by being placed in less-liquid investment solutions. The evidence suggests that the interest of households in deposits is driven more by perceived security and tax treatment than by immediate consumption needs, leading to account balances that are fairly stable over time (BME, 2007; OER, 2011).

Alternatives to bank deposits exist but households may be deterred by several factors that are both subjective – lack of familiarity – and objective – diversity and relative complexity (section 2.1). Long-term investment solutions for retail investors are sometimes scarcely available or are inappropriately labelled. Moreover, following the 2008 crisis, the tightening of prudential requirements is pushing banks to focus sale efforts on deposits (EFAMA, 2011).

Figure 5. Liquidity of European household financial holdings, end 2011 (€ trillion)

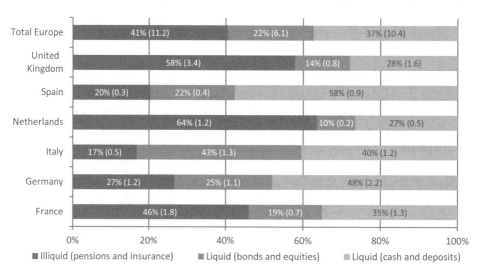

Notes: Total Europe includes Austria, Belgium, Czech Republic, Denmark, Finland, France, Germany, Greece, Hungary, Ireland, Italy, the Netherlands, Norway, Poland, Portugal, Slovak Republic, Spain, Sweden, Switzerland and the UK. Insurance includes life and composite undertakings.

Source: Boston Consulting Group.

Decreasing allocations to equity...

Equity holdings by households decreased by almost 19% in Europe and 14% in the US from 2000 to 2010 (Figure 6). Lower allocations to listed equities can be attributed to a combination of factors, including weaker-than-expected returns, higher volatility and the occurrence of market bubbles (McKinsey, 2011). Retail investors have lost confidence in both stock markets and the asset management value chain (Kay, 2012).[19] Similarly, among institutional investors, awareness of the risks embedded in the provision of guarantees has grown, leading to the generalisation of asset liability management, based primarily on fixed-income rather than equity investments (see EDHEC, 2011).

Perceptions of risks and risk-pricing are also affected by exogenous elements, which shape preferences towards some asset classes to the detriment of others. For instance, taxation in some countries favours investments and financing in debt rather than equity (EC, 2013b). Similarly, explicit and implicit government guarantees favour some instruments, such as retail bank deposits, over others. Prudential rules that are not based on evidence, such as preferential capital charges for sovereign debt, also distort asset allocation (section 1.4).[20] Inducements paid by product originators to distributors can also distort asset allocation.

Lower allocations to risky assets, including equity, by households may increase the likelihood of principal preservation but also entail a lower return potential. In the context of long-term and retirement investing, principal preservation by investing in fixed-income instruments increases pension security but its lower return potential reduces the scope for higher pension adequacy based on yield rather than additional contributions.

---

[19] In the US, a December 2012 survey by the Chicago Booth – Kellogg School 'Financial Trust Index' found that 58% of US citizens saw a fall of more than 30% in equity prices as likely in the following 12 months (http://financialtrustindex.org/). According to this Index, public equity markets are less trusted than banks, mutual funds and large corporations, being in effect the least trusted institution surveyed.

[20] It is also unclear, notably within the Solvency II framework, the extent to which risk charges for less-liquid asset classes reflect risks accurately, as the methodologies typically applied to calculate risk-weights rely on historical market prices, which tend to be less available or informative for these assets, due to their relative illiquidity. On this point see EIOPA (2013e) and EVCA (2012).

Figure 6. Evolution of household financial holdings, 2000-2010

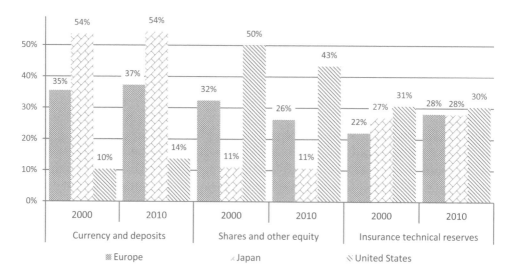

Note: Data from national accounts. Europe includes Austria, Belgium, Czech Republic, Denmark, Estonia, Finland, France, Germany, Greece, Hungary, Italy, the Netherlands, Poland, Portugal, Slovak Republic, Spain, Sweden, the United Kingdom, Norway and Switzerland. See also Table A.1 in the annex.

Source: OECD (2013b).

Poor understanding and risk aversion...

Retail investors and beneficiaries are challenged by the growing diversity and complexity of financial instruments and investment products (IOSCO, 2012), in addition to their own biases and risk aversion (Figure 7). Most individuals are not capable of indentifying the most adequate and cost-effective investment solutions without the assistance of professional and impartial advice.[21] But the cost of such advice is onerous, as it can reduce net returns significantly and act as a barrier for smaller investors to enter the market. Action to address choice and complexity, in addition to disclosure and advice, is hence necessary in the markets for long-term investing and retirement solutions (chapters 2 and 3).

---

[21] Difficulties in choosing are also due to the limited progress achieved on pre-contractual disclosure, beyond the KIID (Key Investor Information Document) for UCITS funds. The proposal to introduce a KID (Key Information Document) for other packaged investment products, including retirement solutions, and potentially also for plain vanilla securities and bonds, aims to introduce a common standard across the board [COM (2012) 352 final].

Figure 7. Risk aversion among retail investors in selected countries

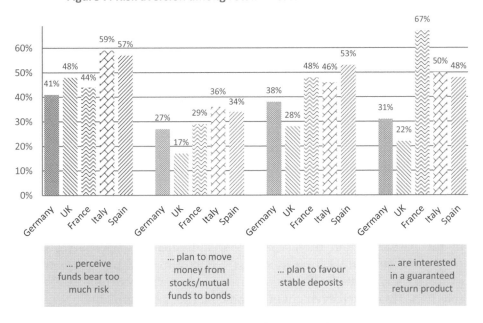

Source: Boston Consulting Group. Data for 2012. See also Figure 12.

Within an incomplete single market...

The markets for retail long-term investment solutions remain mostly national in Europe, in particular for life insurance, pension funds and less-liquid retail investment funds – in contrast with the progress achieved in the cross-border distribution of UCITS. For instance, in 2012 only 84 pension funds operated cross-border in Europe (EIOPA, 2012a), while no EU regulatory framework or marketing passport exists for less-liquid retail investment funds (chapter 2).

A monitoring exercise carried out in 2007 by BME Consulting for the European Commission attributed the low level of integration to: i) the insufficient degree of harmonisation of applicable legislation, ii) the fragmentation of distribution and processing architecture, iii) distortions linked to cross-border taxation, iv) insufficient information and advice regarding product choice and v) limits to the transferability of investments from one product or provider to another.

Of the obstacles to integration above, some have been addressed while others remain largely unaddressed:

⚬ Since the 2008 financial crisis and following the G20 consensus on financial regulation, policy action has focused on building a level playing field across intermediaries in all member states, raising the level of harmonisation in regulation and convergence in supervision. More attention has been paid to the fundamentals of business models, over the traditional categorisation of intermediaries, in an effort to apply consistent rules to equivalent economic functions, reducing the opportunity for arbitrage. Landmarks include the ongoing revision of the rules applicable to insurance companies (Solvency II), occupational pension funds (IORP II) and traditional investment funds (UCITS V/VI), and the introduction of common rules for most other asset management activities (AIFMD).[22] Despite this progress, inconsistencies remain, as well as key gaps, including the absence of an EU framework for personal pensions, which would be central to facilitating retail long-term investing (chapter 3).

○ When it comes to cross-border distribution and investor protection, action has focused on extending disclosure and sale-process requirements across product categories (under the PRIPs initiative).[23] Yet, insufficient ambition in the harmonisation of sale-process requirements is increasing market fragmentation (MiFID II and IMD II).[24] Retail investor protection remains primarily a competence for member states, under the current EU Treaties, which makes the achievement of a single market very difficult.[25]

○ The fragmentation of processing architecture has not been addressed so far, despite its practical importance. In the absence of pan-European processing, subscriptions and redemptions are processed nationally, restricting choice and competition for investors, leading to higher costs and inefficient scale, including for long-term investing purposes. Given path-dependency and coordination costs, the industry is unlikely to find a solution without guidance from regulators. Limits to transferability are closely linked to the absence of standardisation, particularly for less-liquid solutions, in addition to tax obstacles, which also remain largely untackled.[26]

---

[22] Directive 2009/138/EC on the taking-up and pursuit of the business of Insurance and Reinsurance (Solvency II). Directive 2009/65/EC on undertakings for collective investment in transferable securities (UCITS). Proposal for a Directive amending Directive 2009/65/EC as regards depositary functions, remuneration policies and sanctions [COM (2012) 350 final]. Directive 2011/61/EU on Alternative Investment Fund Managers.

[23] Proposal for a Regulation on key information documents for investment products [COM (2012) 352 final].

[24] Proposal for a Directive on markets in financial instruments (MiFID II) [COM (2011) 656 final]. Proposal for a Directive on insurance mediation (IMD II) [COM (2012) 360/2].

[25] Arts 4.2.b and 21.3, Treaty on the Functioning of the European Union.

[26] Amended proposal for a Directive on minimum requirements for enhancing worker mobility by improving the acquisition and preservation of supplementary pension rights (Pension Portability Directive) [COM/2007/603 final].

For reference, Table 2 presents an overview of the regulatory framework for savings solutions in the EU.

Table 2. Overview of the EU regulatory framework for savings solutions

	Selling practices	Pre-contractual disclosure	Asset allocation	Prudential requirements
Deposits (sovereign guarantee)	Local rules	Local rules	Unregulated	CRD IV
Non-guaranteed deposits (< €100k?)	Local rules	Local rules	Unregulated	CRD IV
UCITS	Local rules + MiFID	UCITS KIID	UCITS Directive	UCITS Directive
Other retail investment funds	Local rules + MiFID	(P)RIPs KID	Local rules + AIFMD	Local rules + AIFMD
Life insurance policies/wrappers	Local rules + IMD II	(P)RIPs KID	Solvency II	Solvency II
Personal pensions	Local rules + MiFID	(P)RIPs KID	Local rules	Local rules
Occupational pensions	Local rules (social and labour law)	Local rules [(P)RIPs KID?]	Local rules (IORP I minimum harmonisation)	Local rules (IORP I minimum harmonisation)
Listed securities	Local rules + MiFID	Prospectus Directive [(P)RIPs KID?]	Non-applicable	Non-applicable
Structured products (including deposits)	Local rules + MiFID (new to MiFID II)	(P)RIPs KID	Unregulated	CRD IV (for bank origination)

Source: Author.

1.4　Institutional long-term investing today

Institutional investors are prime long-term investors, but their power to behave as such springs from the long-term horizons of beneficiaries, where they invest for retirement or other consumption needs far off in the future. Life insurers and pension funds are situated therefore at the core of long-term investing.

This section discusses institutional long-term investing today, focusing on the provision of guarantees, the interest of beneficiaries and the impact of changes in macroeconomic conditions and business models. It also considers the role of regulation and the ongoing reform of the prudential framework for insurers and pension funds in Europe.

Linked to the provision of guarantees...

The business of life insurers and pension funds has been traditionally linked to the provision of guarantees, that is, the protection of the capital invested and the promise of a given return or income stream, whereby the provider (on its own or with a sponsor) assumes market and other risks (such as longevity risk) on its balance sheet. It is estimated that nearly 65% of assets held by European life insurers are backing policies that offer some form of guarantee (€3 trillion) – the remaining 35% being invested for the benefit of policyholders who bear market risk in full (€1.7 trillion) (EIOPA, 2012, Table 6).[27] Similarly, pension funds have been traditionally linked to the provision of guarantees. In 2011, 80% of assets under management by autonomous pension funds in Europe were deemed to belong to defined benefit (DB) schemes (€3 trillion).[28] However, even DB funds increasingly incorporate risk pass-through mechanisms (EIOPA, 2012c).

Non-guaranteed insurance policies and pension schemes are pure investment management products, where the full market risk falls on the investor, similar to the retail investment funds which frequently serve as the underlying. Hybrid schemes share the market or other risks between the provider and the beneficiary. Figures 8 and 9 present the business composition of life insurance and pension funds in Europe.

Figure 8. Composition of the business of life insurers in EU-27, 2003-11 (€ trillion)

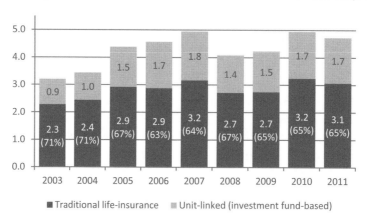

■ Traditional life-insurance   ■ Unit-linked (investment fund-based)

Source: EIOPA (2012a).

---

[27] Approximately a further €0.2 trillion is invested for the benefit of policyholders who bear market risk in full by 'composite' undertakings (insurers combining life and non-life business). The share of life versus non-life insurance within composite undertakings is however not apparent in the available statistics. Supposing both business lines weigh equally, an additional €0.7 trillion would be invested by European insurers in connection to traditional life insurance offering some form of guarantee.

[28] Author's own elaboration based on Towers Watson, BCG and OECD data. The remaining assets were managed by defined contribution (DC) (16% or €0.6 trillion) and hybrid schemes (4% or €0.15 trillion). Additional €2.2 trillion were held in book reserves by non-autonomous pensions funds (mostly defined benefit).

Figure 9. Composition of the business of occupational pension funds in selected European countries, 2011

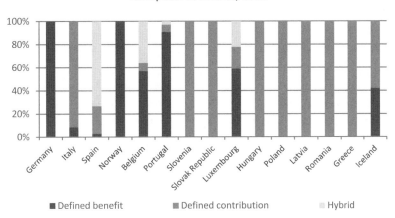

Source: Data compiled by EIOPA (2012b) on a best-effort basis an approximate view of the financial position of occupational pension funds during 2011.

Guarantees provide a useful social function as they increase pension safety and help mitigate income inequality at retirement. Investors are given assurances as to the level of benefits and are protected against untimely drops in asset prices. The relevance of guarantees within personal pensions is framed by the overall pension and social security system in each country – automatic stabilisers and public anti-poverty schemes are alternatives to guarantees in private pensions (OECD, 2012).

The guarantees linked to different life insurance policies and pension contracts are not homogeneous but depend, first and foremost, on the risks covered and, for similar risk coverage, on the level of return promised. Product choice varies across member states depending on market development and regulation.[29] The differences ultimately relate to two respects: i) whether the provider assumes only market risk – protecting initial capital and delivering a fixed return – or also longevity risk – delivering an income until death, potentially exceeding the capital accumulated (as in annuities and defined benefit pension schemes); and ii) whether the risks are assumed by the provider in full or the insurance policy/pension contract foresees any risk pass-through mechanisms, whereby certain risks are shared with the beneficiaries or a sponsor.[30]

---

[29] For instance, in some member states occupational pension funds are obliged to be defined benefit.

[30] Guarantees can also be classified with respect to whether they are: i) set on nominal or real terms, ii) set as fixed or minimum return, iii) provided for a definite or indefinite period of time and iv) final or resettable during the application period (OECD, 2012, p. 135).

But widely heterogeneous guarantees...

As just noted, the guarantees offered in the marketplace are heterogeneous, not only as to their level but also with respect to their supporting features. The presence of a sponsor (typically the employer) is a salient supporting feature, which typically differentiates life insurance and defined benefit pension funds. Where a sponsor is present, market and other risks are not borne solely by the pension fund but also by the employer, in accordance with national law and the contract with beneficiaries. The pension promise is therefore supported not only by the financial strength of the fund but also by that of the sponsor.[31]

Similarly, under compulsory participation, pension funds usually also have the ability to raise contributions. In a collective scheme, if redistribution of risk and funding among generations is allowed, additional contributions from current employees may be used to fund ongoing benefits (to current retirees), which may operate as an additional support to the guarantee provided.[32]

In addition to their supporting features, guarantees are also characterised by their level of strictness. Both pension funds and insurance policies increasingly incorporate risk pass-through mechanisms allowing for benefit cuts, chiefly in case of underfunding. Where contracts incorporate risk pass-through clauses in the exceptional circumstances (such as high risk of bankruptcy of the undertaking), they may still be considered to provide a guarantee. However, if the guarantee is framed or made contingent on market indicators (such as market interest rates or stock indices) the contract should rather be considered as a 'hybrid'.

Demanding distinct investment practices...

The provision of guarantees requires the implementation of specific investment practices (asset-liability management) and prudential safeguards (regulatory capital and supervision), which become more relevant, the stricter the guarantee. Asset-liability management (ALM) and liability-driven investment (LDI) try to match asset allocation with the expected profile of liability cash-flows in order to generate returns that are similar to those liabilities in volume and timing. It requires the estimation of the profile of future liabilities, which

---

[31] Similar to the support provided by a sponsor, mutual insurers may call for supplementary contributions from their members.

[32] The guarantee offered by current employees to current retirees needs to be balanced against the need to fund the future pensions of current employees, which depends both on their own contributions and those of future employees. So-called 'intergenerational solidarity' in collective schemes may be welfare enhancing but is affected by constraints, given the uncertainty surrounding future contributions and returns, in later generations. See Beetsma et al. (2011), Hollanders (2010) and Gollier (2008).

may be subject to uncertainty, for instance where benefits are inflation-indexed or the provider bears the longevity risk. It leads to an asset allocation with a similar pattern of returns and life-cycle to the liabilities it backs.

Where long-term guarantees are provided, ALM is typically based on either cash-flow or duration matching.[33] Fixed-income assets are used because of the characteristics they share with the liabilities arising from the provision of long-term guarantees, in terms of surety, predictability of cash-flows and sensitivity to interest rates. Where assets are held to maturity and offer an income stream in line with the liabilities they back, the likelihood of meeting these liabilities is high (except if the issuer defaults) and spread risk will be mitigated or, in case of perfect matching, eliminated.[34]

ALM strategies under long-term investment horizons are inherently conducive to long-term investing as assets with long life-cycles (in particular fixed-income instruments) are held over long periods of time or to maturity, providing long-term and stable funding to issuers. Limits to cash flow and duration matching arise, however, from the difficult modelling of some liabilities, limited supply of assets with long enough maturities and rebalancing of portfolios as the yield curve moves. Regular rebalancing is needed as the yield curve does not usually move in parallel but becomes flatter or steeper, leading to maturity mismatches (Morgan Stanley, 2013).

Where a sponsor backs the guarantee afforded to members (partly or fully, as per the sponsorship arrangement or the law) or risk pass-through mechanisms are present in the pension contract with current and future beneficiaries, an ALM framework remains best practice. But the backstops provided allow this framework to depart from the strict matching of assets and liabilities based on fixed-income instruments and to assume additional equity and equity-like risk, with potentially higher returns (Amenc et al., 2009).

And prudential safeguards...

The provision of guarantees also necessitates prudential safeguards, namely regulatory capital requirements and close supervision of the business practices (promised returns for new contracts) and funding position of the provider with

---

[33] Cash-flow matching involves investing in fixed-income instruments whose pattern of returns (coupons) matches a given liability stream. Duration matching involves investing in fixed-income instruments whose interest-rate sensitivity (the sensitivity to a parallel shift in the yield curve) is equivalent to that of the liabilities matched.

[34] Perfect matching is rarely possible in practice given the practical limitations explained later in this report.

respect to the liabilities in its balance sheet.[35] The function of regulatory capital is to cover the likely losses in tail events to which the provider of the guarantee is exposed – for instance, issuer default in case of assets held to maturity or a deep drop in market values, when liabilities become due, for equity holdings. Capital also reflects the risks linked to the modelling of liabilities – for instance, longer than modelled life expectancies if longevity risk rests with the provider.

Regulatory capital increases the likelihood of meeting liabilities, including in adverse market conditions, but constrains investment practices and carries an economic cost.[36] Guarantees do, however, play a useful function in increasing the security of retirement income and facilitating voluntary participation by risk-adverse investors in retirement-savings vehicles.

Investment practices and prudential safeguards are inter-linked in two ways: i) since regulatory capital should reflect the risks that the provider is effectively exposed to, capital requirements need to factor in investment practices, to the extent that they shape those risks; and ii) investment restrictions can be foregone as long as appropriate capitalisation is provided (see below).[37]

Conversely, in the absence of any guarantee, where market and other risks are borne by the investor, no capital requirements should apply (except to cover operational risks). Such is the instance of unit-linked insurance policies[38] and defined contribution pension schemes. In the absence of guarantees and capital burdens, these products are able to maximise the share of principal invested and have the freedom to invest in more-risky assets, potentially offering higher

---

[35] Supervision is geared to ensure that providers do not offer new guarantees to consumers who are unlikely to be fulfilled under projected market yields (in particular long-term interest rates). It is also directed at monitoring the funding of liabilities in the balance sheet and, in the event of underfunding, triggering remedial action.

[36] The cost of a guarantee is the risk margin which, on top of the best estimate, is equal to the present value of the costs, for the undertaking, of holding regulatory capital in relation to it.

[37] The introduction of Solvency II and other risk-based prudential and supervisory frameworks aims at drawing the link between regulatory capital and investment practices, lifting previously generalised investment restrictions. Solvency II allows insurers to invest in any asset class, including equities and less-liquid assets, as far as sufficient capital is set aside. It may not, however, fully reflect the effect that ALM practices have in shaping the risks borne by the insurer.

[38] Unit-linked products (insurance policies) are packaged retail investment products (PRIPs, as defined by European Commission, 2009) which are distributed and/or created by an insurance undertaking but offer no insurance guarantee and have units or shares of a collective investment undertaking as underlying. Pure unit-linked products, where the full market risk is borne by the policy-holder and no ancillary insurance cover is provided, are exempt from capital requirements for market risk under Solvency II but are subject to requirements for operational risk and expense risk (Art. 105).

returns. Nevertheless, if the objective is to build retirement income, the potential for a higher return should be balanced against the need to mitigate risks. Risk mitigation in the context of retirement savings, even in the absence of a guarantee, calls for the implementation of an ALM framework.

A customised and hybrid approach, both in terms of investment practices and prudential framework, is better adapted to the provision of limited guarantees (under risk pass-through exceptions), which are based on market indicators (interest rates or equity indices) or endorsed by a sponsor. As for investment practices, these products may also invite investments in asset classes that are different from fixed-income, with a long-term life cycle but a higher potential return. And capital requirements should account for any limits introduced to the guarantee and/or any sponsoring arrangement, as well as the financial soundness of the sponsor.

Adapting to low interest rates...

Unconventional monetary policies in developed economies following the 2008 financial crisis and the ongoing economic downturn have brought interest rates to historical lows. Interest rates have been close to zero in nominal terms and negative in real terms since 2009. As the processes of bank and public-sector deleveraging continue in most developed economies, and economic growth and job creation remain elusive, unconventional monetary policies are expected to continue in the future (EIOPA, 2013; ECB, 2013).

The provision of long-term guarantees is directly affected by interest rates, as it is mostly supported by fixed-income investments. The impact of a prolonged period of low interest rates on the provision of guarantees is better described by distinguishing between legacy and new liabilities. Existing or legacy liabilities, priced on the estimated term structure of interest rates[39] at issuance, need to be fulfilled, even if the yield curve would later on be radically altered (as far as no risk pass-through exceptions are foreseen). By way of illustration, a traditional life insurance policy sold in 2004 offered a guarantee based on an interest rate for long maturities nearing 5%, while in 2013, the yield curve exhibits long-term rates below 3%, in spite of which the original guarantee would need to be fulfilled (Figure 10).

---

[39] The term structure of interest rates (also known as yield curve) represents the relationship between interest rates (market remuneration or asset pricing) and the remaining time to maturity of debt securities. The forward yield curve presents the short-term interest rate for future periods implied in the spot yield curve.

Figure 10. Euro-area yield curve (illustrative spread 2004-13)

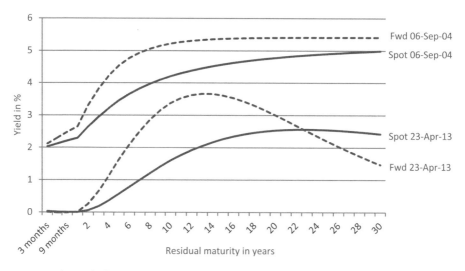

Note: The graph plots spot and instantaneous forward yield curves for AAA-rated euro-area central government bonds, drawing on earliest and latest dates for which the yield curves were available at the time of drafting.

Source: ECB Statistical Data Warehouse (2013).

Providers, however, are not fully exposed to the risk above. In particular, asset-liability management (ALM) allows the provision of long-term guarantees, by mitigating interest-rate risk via cash flow and maturity matching. Albeit, since perfect matching is not possible – especially for longer-term liabilities given the limited supply of corresponding assets – providers are partially exposed to a decline in interest rates, notably through reinvestment risk. This exposure to interest-rate risk varies greatly across intermediaries but may not be fully apparent, depending on accounting and reporting practices (EIOPA, 2013a). On average in 2012, European insurers were estimated to maintain reasonable margins between the guarantees on their balance sheets and the average return on the assets backing them (Figure 11). Bonds purchased when interest rates were higher than today have probably not matured yet but the pressure on margins (and ultimately on capital) may later materialise depending on duration gaps and the persistence of low rates.

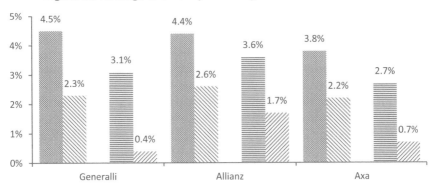

Figure 11. Average and new yields vs. guarantees in life insurance

≋ Running yield ⟍ Average guarantee in force ≡ New money yield ⧄ Average new guarantee

Source: Morgan Stanley (2013), based on company data for 2012.

To service legacy liabilities in a prolonged low interest-rate environment, it is possible that insurers and pension funds will moderately re-risk, in the search for yield, increasing their allocations to equity and less-liquid asset classes, in spite of the comparatively higher capital charges applicable under forthcoming regulations, such as Solvency II (BlackRock, 2012). There is evidence that insurers run higher risks in some jurisdictions, notably the US (Box 1). In sum, low interest rates present challenges to the servicing of legacy liabilities.

When it comes to new business, insurers and pensions funds are framing their guarantees in line with (lower) projected rates of return and introducing risk pass-through mechanisms. These institutional investors realise that market conditions may change in unforeseeable ways, particularly over the long-term horizons that are typical of the provision of guarantees in retirement-savings products. In effect, product offerings and business models are evolving towards the provision of more limited guarantees. The next subsection considers this transition.

Box 1. Impact of low interest rates on solvency and financial stability

The potential impact of a prolonged period of low interest rates on the solvency position of life insurers and some defined-benefit pension funds is of great concern to supervisors (EIOPA, 2012c). This concern is generally more acute for insurers, given the absence of sponsoring entities (i.e. employers), which are typically present in occupational pension schemes. This condition also exposes funds less directly to competition from alternative providers of retirement-savings solutions. The case of Japan, where seven life insurers failed at the end of the 1990s, is frequently cited as an example of the risks posed by low interest rates to financial stability. We consider these respects in more detail below.

Persistently low interest rates may impact the (future) solvency position of insurers and pension funds where assets are not fully matched to liabilities, resulting in heightened reinvestment risk, that is, the risk that future interest rates would be below the rate of return promised to policy-holders: When the duration of existing liabilities exceeds that of the assets backing them, insurers and funds have to reinvest upon maturity (or earlier). Persistently low interest rates make it unlikely that new investments offer a rate of return above the one guaranteed to beneficiaries, putting pressure on the profitability of insurers (and pension funds) and ultimately on their solvency position.

Depending on the reporting and accounting methodology employed by the life insurer or pension fund, the impact of low rates may not be immediately apparent. Under mark-to-market prospective accounting, low interest rates would increase the present value of liabilities, resulting in an instantaneous deterioration of the (reported) solvency position. Yet, this deterioration may be artificial if it fails to take into account the extent of interest-rate risk immunisation obtained through asset-liability management practices (discussed in more detail in section 1.4).

Moreover, as life insurers (and pension funds) move towards lower or limited guarantees, they will be more exposed to competition from pure asset managers (investment funds), banks (deposits, structured products) and direct holdings (bonds, shares). The change in business model may result in further pressure on profitability; although non-guaranteed products are today more profitable than guaranteed ones, the situation is likely to change as competition toughens. In sum, the traditional value proposition of insurers may suffer, resulting in downward pressures on sales and profits, with potentially adverse consequences for the servicing of legacy liabilities (EIOPA, 2013a).

EIOPA (2013) advises market participants and national supervisors to look at a wide range of risk metrics, based both on market value and historical cost accounting, as well as cash flow and its evolution. It encourages supervisors to demand increased provisioning for existing business and to monitor new product offerings, in order to ensure that guarantees are not set at levels that are unlikely to be met, challenging business models where appropriate.

Persistently low interest rates may also drive insurers and pension funds to increase the risk in their portfolios. The effect of moderate re-risking should not be detrimental per se to policy-holders or financial stability, as long as appropriate capitalisation is provided, in line with the risks of the assets held. In this respect, EIOPA has urged the introduction of the risk-based capital charges and prudential controls in Solvency II (Bernardino, 2012). It has also put forward a plan to introduce the principles of risk-based supervision before the formal adoption of the legislation (EIOPA, 2012d). The IMF (2013) has warned of substantial re-risking and even 'gambling for resurrection' among defined benefit pension funds and life insurers in the US, which European providers seem to have eschewed so far. In Europe, the discussion is focused on whether the precise capital charges envisaged under Solvency II accurately reflect the relevant risks.

When considering financial stability, banks attract the most attention but the likelihood and potential impact of widespread failures among insurers and pension funds should not be underestimated. A prolonged period of low interest rates caused the failure of seven life insurers in Japan between 1997 and 2001 and forced the adoption of legislation allowing defaults on guarantees (EIOPA, 2013a). The Japanese crisis, however, was not only caused by persistently low interest rates but also by the continuation of unsustainable business models – offering disproportionate guarantees for new policies, in an environment of intense competition among intermediaries and inactive supervision – inadequate investment practices and a very sharp decline in stock market prices – down by 60% in Tokyo (CGFS, 2011).

In transition to limited guarantees...

Our focus in 2012 was on developing and rolling out our defined contribution product range, including a new mutual fund range with a transparent and low cost structure, while continuing to cut costs and look for efficiencies across our operations. We remain cautious of defined benefit products, which we view as unsustainable for both employers and insurers, and continued to withdraw from guaranteed products where customers were not prepared to pay the increased market consistent costs of guarantees. [...] We also launched a new product that provides customers with a guaranteed return linked to the market interest rate, rather than a fixed percentage guarantee.

Excerpt from the 2012 Annual Report of Achmea,
a major insurer from the Netherlands (p. 42).

As reflected in the excerpt above, a prolonged period of low interest rates could accelerate the transition in product and business models towards limited and no guarantees. Non-guaranteed and hybrid life insurance policies and pension schemes are growing in volume and market share, a trend supported by both regulation and consumer preferences (EIOPA, 2012c). This move, however, is not only explained by low interest rates but also by a number of diverse reasons, in a manner similar to the transition from defined benefit to defined contribution pension schemes, which has been well documented (OECD, 2012):

- *Potentially higher returns for investors,* as there is more flexibility to allocate investments to equities and less-liquid asset classes – a potential that becomes more likely in the context of low interest rates.

- *Simpler regulatory framework and easier administration,* given the absence of the prudential requirements typically linked to the provision of guarantees.

- *Higher profitability for intermediaries,* measured as return on equity (Morgan Stanley, 2013), given both lower capital intensity and competition dynamics in the marketplace.

- *Higher certainty for employers* (plan sponsors) as to the timing and volume of their commitments and liabilities.

- *Sometimes easier transferability for employees* (ease of changing providers), better adapted to growing career and geographical mobility in labour markets.

- *Higher perceived transparency and sense of immediacy,* given easier access to the value of accumulated savings and returns.

Guarantees are beneficial for pension safety (see above) but also entail costs, depending on their level and characteristics. The OECD (2012) estimates that a guarantee covering the principal invested (nominal at retirement) has a yearly cost of 1.24% of contributions or 0.06% of accumulated net asset value.[40] This estimation is inherently sensitive to the contribution period, investment strategy and capital-market conditions. For instance, a parallel shift in the yield curve (see above) of -1% would increase the cost cited above to 4.2% of contributions. A higher allocation to equities, instead of bonds, would also increase the cost. Moreover, these are estimations of the nominal cost (similar to a premium), which do not comprise the compound loss on foregone contributions, since the premium paid is not accumulated in the scheme and does not generate returns.

Higher guarantees carry higher nominal costs, as shown in Table 3. The table also provides an overview of the benefits of guarantees for beneficiaries: the probability that the final lump sum received by the investor at 65 is higher, having selected an option with guarantee, rather than the lump sum s/he would have received if a non-guaranteed option had been selected. This probability may also be seen as a proxy for the trade-off between pension security and adequacy.

---

[40] The estimations provided by the OECD (2012) are for guarantees offered (as an option) within defined contribution pension schemes. Within defined benefit pension and traditional life insurance, (risk-based) capital requirements similarly account for the nominal cost of the guarantees provided.

Table 3. Mean nominal costs and benefits of guarantees

	Fees paid as % of lump sum at 65	Loss as % in lump sum at 65	Probability guarantee is exercised	Probability higher lump sum
Capital guarantee (at retirement)	00.86	01.28	00.49	00.48
Inflation-indexed capital guarantee	03.67	05.49	06.48	05.22
Ongoing capital guarantee	06.08	07.14	83.45	18.20
Floating guarantee (1-year interest rate)	15.96	23.81	40.33	21.72
4% guarantee (with annual fees)	12.20	18.30	35.32	21.26

Source: OECD (2012, pp. 129-151).

The development of retirement solutions offering limited or no guarantees, however, is held back (to some extent myopically) by risk aversion among potential beneficiaries. Despite the high cost of guarantees (not always made apparent to investors) and the decrease in promised returns (given low rates), consumers are unwilling to take on market risk. Non-guaranteed products therefore lack traction among investors in key markets. Figure 12 presents consumer perceptions in major European economies, showing that risk aversion is on the rise, probably due still to the loss of confidence in financial intermediation and the ongoing uncertainty surrounding global imbalances. In 2012, about 43% of European investors were likely to favour a guaranteed over a non-guaranteed product. However, the ratio varied greatly across countries, reflecting different traditions and risk perceptions – nearly 20% in the UK versus 60% in France.

Figure 12. Evolution of risk aversion in Europe, 2010-12

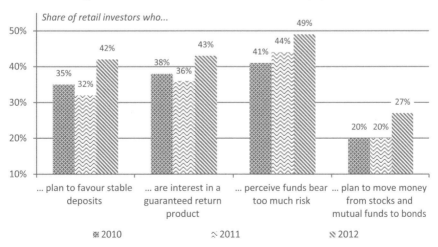

Note: See also Figure 7 for more information on risk aversion in Europe.
Source: Boston Consulting Group.

From the perspective of long-term investing, the management of savings pools that do not incorporate guarantees has a higher potential, given the additional flexibility in terms of asset allocation and the inherently long-term investment horizons linked to the accumulation of pension savings. Asset allocation may indeed deviate from fixed-income with more freedom than would otherwise be permissible if guarantees were present. Higher allocation to equity is hence possible, and may be desirable, given potentially higher returns for investors. However, the potential for long-term investing in equities[41] would not be fully exploited unless the liquidity profile of product units (in terms of redemptions) is in line with the long-term horizon inherent in investing for retirement. If this condition is fulfilled, a higher allocation to less-liquid asset classes, with equity -like characteristics would also be possible. Section 1.1 considers the definition of long-term investing with reference to asset classes and investment practices, and the liquidity profile of retail investment products. Chapter 3 considers how to align solution design and market structure, in the provision of personal DC pension plans, with long-term investing.

The potential for higher allocations to equity in the absence of guarantees is shown in Figure 13. In effect, the average allocation to equity in defined contribution schemes is twice as big if they do not incorporate guarantees. Similarly, in most countries with both DB and DC schemes, equity allocation tends to be higher in the latter – notably in the US, DC 401ks plans allocate 60% to equities, in contrast to 40% in corporate pension funds (Severinson & Yermo, 2012, p. 27). However, in Europe, the largest DC schemes allocate 22% to equities while the largest DB schemes allocate 35%, a phenomenon that can be attributed to risk aversion among investors (McKinsey, 2011, p. 31).[42]

---

[41] Long-term investing in equity instruments is defined in this report as strategic, low turnover and engaged holdings (see section 1.1, chapter 1).

[42] In contrast with defined benefit plans, in most defined contribution plans, investors are given a choice in terms of asset allocation, which explains the relevance of investor preferences and risk aversion.

Figure 13. Asset allocation in defined contribution schemes in OECD countries, 2011

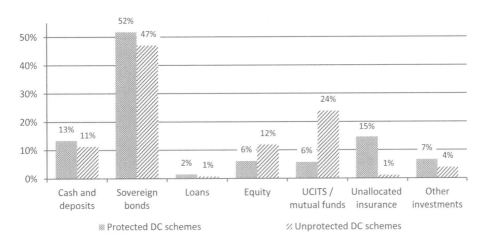

Source: OECD Statistics.

Awaiting regulatory change...

Life insurers and defined benefit pension funds are awaiting the introduction of a comprehensive prudential and supervisory framework in Europe, based on a total (or holistic) balance-sheet approach – which considers the risks presented by both assets and liabilities – and prospective market consistent valuations. These changes are expected to be introduced by two separate pieces of legislation, for insurers (Solvency II) and occupational pension funds (IORP II, under study) – given the important differences in product features, business models, operations and risks between these two sorts of entities (see above).

Solvency II was adopted in November 2009, but its provisions have not been implemented yet. Shortly following its adoption, a review process was initiated to adapt it to the changes introduced by the Lisbon Treaty for implementing legislation and the creation of EIOPA (European Insurance and Occupational Pensions Authority). What was initially envisaged as a narrow and technical revision, however, was extended in scope to include material changes to the framework.

Further analysis of the impact of Solvency II raised several issues of concern, which prompted a reassessment of the scope of the changes needed before the regime could be implemented in practice. These concerns included, notably, the extent to which, by not properly recognising the effects of asset-liability management (ALM) practices, Solvency II could undermine the provision of guarantees by life insurers and introduce artificial volatility in technical provisions, available capital and regulatory capital requirements.

At the same time, the European Commission has announced the revision of the 2003 Directive on IORPs (institutions for occupational retirement provision), which is expected to follow broadly similar principles to the regulation of life insurance. The legislative proposal has not yet been issued, notably due to the diversity of business models among pension funds and institutional settings at national level, which makes it difficult to devise homogenous rules. Qualitative aspects (governance and disclosure) will be reviewed first, while the merits behind introducing harmonised quantitative requirements (regulatory capital) will receive further analysis (European Commission, 2013c; EIOPA, 2013b).

Both reforms, however, affect the provision of guarantees for long-term savings and share the objective of strengthening the resilience of insurance and pension-fund undertakings, thereby protecting beneficiaries and financial stability. But they are also aimed at overcoming regulatory fragmentation among member states, furthering European market integration and benefits for consumers. In some member states, Solvency II and IORP II will entail a complete overhaul of existing regulations and supervisory practices, while in others, risk-based supervision is already in place.

The following sections consider the main features of the Solvency II framework and the key points of contention, which have delayed its introduction. Section 2.2 considers the review of the IORP Directive, from a single market perspective.

What is Solvency II?

Solvency II consists of the recasting of fourteen insurance directives, together with the introduction of risk-based prudential requirements and an accompanying supervisory framework for insurance and reinsurance undertakings, both life and non-life (European Commission, 2008).

The stated objectives of Solvency II are, firstly, the protection of policy-holders, and only secondarily, other goals such as financial stability or the promotion of fair and stable markets (Preamble 16 and Article 27). Long-term investing is not among the objectives pursued by Solvency II and it probably should not be, to the extent that it is defined as gross capital formation without direct connection with the interest of beneficiaries. Yet, it should strive to promote investment practices aligned with the long-term horizons of liabilities in life insurance.[43]

---

[43] Holding long-term investments is a straightforward way to comply with the requirement to cover the insurance liabilities in a manner appropriate to the nature and duration of those liabilities (Article 132.2 paragraph 3, Solvency II). For a discussion on the concept of long-term investing and the position of beneficiaries, see section 1.1 of chapter 1 in this report.

The framework is best understood by referring to three pillars: i) *quantitative requirements* – minimum and solvency capital calculations and thresholds; ii) *qualitative requirements* – governance, risk management and supervision; and iii) *reporting and disclosure* – publicly and privately to supervisors. But it also addresses solvency and supervision at group level and recasts legislation on the reorganisation or winding-up (liquidation) of failing insurers, among other important aspects.

○ *Quantitative requirements* are based on a total balance sheet approach, aimed at factoring all risks both on the asset and liability side of the balance sheet, and their interrelations. It applies therefore capital charges that depend both on market (investments falling in value) and underwriting risks (liabilities being higher than expected or contributions lower). The insurer is required to hold sufficient own funds to cover a 'solvency capital requirement' (SCR) in proportion to the present value of its business (technical provisions). The Directive defines the methodology to calculate the present value of business, which is modelled and then discounted at the risk-free rate (term structure). Valuations are forward-looking and market-consistent – Solvency II does not regulate accounting but is meant to be in line with internationally accepted standards (IFRS and IAS). A standard formula is used to calculate the SCR, unless the insurer applies to its supervisor for the recognition of an internal model. Internal models are expected to be approved only if they provide a better reflection of the specific risks linked to the product mix and business model of the insurer. However, capital charges for each asset class are in principle assigned by the regulator, who will calibrate charges periodically, based on historical data. When capital falls below the SCR, remedial action needs to be taken, based upon a more in-depth assessment, in coordination with the supervisor. The SCR is devised to act as an early warning mechanism; ultimate supervisory action, such as transfer or liquidation, would be undertaken only if an insurer falls below a 'minimum capital requirement' (MCR).

○ *Qualitative requirements* provide the counterbalance to the mechanical use of historical data to calculate risk weights and capital charges. Insurers have to put in place qualitative risk management processes and, most importantly, conduct a so-called 'own risk and solvency assessment' (ORSA) regularly. ORSAs are expected to become an integral part of the business strategy and inform all strategic decisions by the insurer. They will notably provide the framework for stress tests and analysis of deviations between the real risk profile of the insurer and the assumptions underlying the standard formula for the SCR. ORSAs are also a supervisory tool. Solvency II creates a 'supervisory review process' (SRP) aimed at a closer monitoring and deeper understanding not only of financial indicators but also of business model dynamics. The process should result in early intervention at different intensity levels ('supervisory ladder') well before insolvency would materialise.

∘ *Reporting and disclosure* obligations are aimed both at fostering transparency, comparability and market discipline, and at equipping supervisors with the information they need to perform effective supervision. Insurers are notably required to publicly disclose abundant information, periodically and in case of significant developments, such as non-compliance with the MCR or SCR.

Experts and industry participants broadly recognise the merits of Solvency II but questions remain as to whether it accurately reflects the characteristics and risks linked to the provision of (life) insurance.[44] Many insurers in Europe are already operating internal models and governance structures that are similar to those put forward by Solvency II (Morgan Stanley, 2013). And it is generally acknowledged to be leading the process towards greater sophistication in risk management and investment practices – even before entering into force.

The industry has been particularly keen to implement the principles informing Solvency II, given the shortcomings in the previous framework: Solvency I does not account for risks on the asset side of the balance sheet (and only partially on the liability side), while unduly restricting eligible investments and failing to address governance and risk management. Furthermore, it does not supply supervisors with sufficient information to perform their functions and it does not provide the level of harmonisation needed within a single market.

Delays in Solvency II are keeping life insurers and supervisors badly equipped to deal with the challenges derived from low interest rates and volatile market conditions (EIOPA, 2013a; S&P, 2013).[45] This has prompted EU supervisors to agree to the early introduction of its principles, even before the legislation is formally implemented. In particular, national supervisors are working with undertakings to ensure that effective risk-management processes are put in place, including a forward-looking assessment of own risks, similar to the ORSAs (EIOPA, 2012c and 2013b)

Despite wide acknowledgement of the need to implement Solvency II, industry and stakeholders have expressed concerns about parts of the framework, which has prompted its review before it is fully applied in practice. The next

---

[44] For a discussion of the business model of life insurers and the provision of guarantees, including investment practices and prudential requirements, please refer to the subsections above.

[45] For a discussion of the impact of the expected period of persistently low interest rates on the business and solvency of life insurers and financial stability, please refer to Box 1 and the subsections above.

section considers the key points of contention, discussed by Task Force members at the meetings. Before considering those points, Table 4 presents a summary of the three pillars of Solvency II and their main provisions.

Table 4. Overview of the Solvency II framework

PILLAR I **Quantitative Requirements**	PILLAR II **Qualitative Requirements**	PILLAR III **Reporting and Disclosure**
◦ Economic risk-based capital charges	◦ General governance requirements	◦ Annual report on solvency and financial condition
◦ Solvency (ongoing) and minimum capital thresholds	◦ Risk management and compliance functions	◦ Ongoing public disclosure obligations
◦ Classification of own funds according to loss absorption	◦ Internal audit and actuarial functions	◦ Additional reporting to supervisors
◦ Valuation of assets, liabilities and technical provisions	◦ Own-risk and solvency assessments	**OTHER ASPECTS**
◦ Appraisal of risk-mitigation and diversification effects	◦ Separate management of life and non-life business	◦ Group solvency / supervision
◦ Symmetric adjustment to capital charges for equities	◦ Supervisory review process and intervention ladder	◦ Winding-up / re-organisation
◦ Adjustment to the discount rate for matched liabilities	◦ Recovery plans and finance schemes	◦ Limits on investment restrictions / capital add-ons
		◦ Provisions for specific insurance contracts

Source: Author, based on Directive.

Points of contention in Solvency II

Solvency II will bring a sea change to regulation and supervision of insurance in Europe. It has naturally raised concerns and opposition from various angles and stakeholders. This report focuses on the prospective impact of selected aspects of Solvency II on asset allocation and the ability of life insurers to invest in line with the long-term investment horizons of beneficiaries, in the context of long-term (retirement) savings products.[46]

◦ *The use of short-term horizons for the calibration of capital charges*

The solvency capital requirement (SCR) is determined as the capital needed to limit the probability that an insurer will fail to 1 in 200 chances during a year. It is calculated using a value-at-risk measure calibrated at a 99.5% confidence level over a 12-month horizon (Article 101). The calibration of

---

[46] By extension, some of the aspects discussed here may be relevant for defined benefit pension funds as well, under IORP II. The IORP II directive being however in a study phase, it is difficult to anticipate its content.

capital charges for the different asset classes is therefore based on this yearly horizon.

However, when an investor faces a long-term liability profile and has hence the ability to hold assets over several years, the use of a 12-month horizon to calibrate capital charges may fail to capture the risks effectively run by the insurer, while possibly over-representing the impact of short-term volatility on asset prices.

It is suggested that the horizon for the calibration of capital charges should instead be in line with their life cycle. This is of particular relevance for less-liquid asset classes, where the absence of liquid secondary markets means that the investor is effectively tied to holding the assets until they mature.

○ *The steepness of capital charges with regard to duration and rating*

Capital charges under Solvency II increase with longer durations and lower ratings, given higher credit risk (the risk that the issuer would default). The steepness of this increase is a matter of concern to the extent that: i) long-term liabilities are typically better served by investing in instruments with longer, rather than shorter, maturities; and ii) top-rated assets have become more scarce, following the financial and sovereign debt crisis. Box 2 (below) considers more broadly the influence of the standard capital charges under Solvency II on asset allocation.

○ *The likely unintended effects of zero risk-weights for sovereign debt*[47]

The award of zero risk-weights to sovereign debt is unwarranted by actual developments, including recent debt restructuring in Europe. At a macroeconomic level, it results in the crowding-out of resources that could otherwise be available to the private sector, and may result in lower potential growth, in particular for countries with high debt levels – also lowering the incentives for fiscal consolidation. At a micro level, it distorts the asset allocation process, pursued by insurers in the interest of beneficiaries, to the detriment of any other asset class with a similar risk profile but higher capital charges – despite possibly a higher return, which is more beneficial to investors.

Zero capital charges for sovereigns are notably expected to deter investment in debt issued by corporations. However, preferences would also be shaped by other factors, including the supply of sufficiently long maturities, relative returns and correlations with other asset classes. Unintended effects may include higher access to riskier assets, which are worse suited to

---

[47] Note, however, that capital charges for interest rate risk apply to sovereign bonds.

meeting guaranteed returns, but may offset the meagre returns typically offered by government bonds (Morgan Stanley, 2013).

Applying capital charges to sovereign debt is not straightforward, both due to the potential impact in funding costs for sovereigns and the difficulty in finding the right weighting. However, the potential unintended effects just cited invite the phased introduction of risk weights, as proposed by the Group of Thirty (2013).

○ *Sometimes inaccurate reflection of business models and risks*

The provision of guarantees, within long-term (retirement) savings products by life insurers, is understood to necessitate the implementation of specific investment practices, broadly known as asset-liability management (ALM). These practices try to match asset allocation with the profile of liabilities in order to minimise interest-rate and re-investment risks, by investing in assets with a similar pattern of returns and life-cycle to the liabilities they back.[48]

By not fully recognising the risk-mitigation effects of these strategies, it is feared that Solvency II may distort asset allocation and risk management, or otherwise unduly increase the cost of providing guarantees in this context. Central to this discussion is the extent to which the standard formula under Solvency II recognises interest-risk immunisation and distinguishes spread from default risk, as considered below in more detail.

○ *Artificial volatility in balance sheets and reported solvency positions*

Solvency II is based on prospective and market-consistent valuation of both assets and liabilities. However, where the valuation does not recognise the effects of spread-risk immunisation, it may lead to artificial volatility in balance sheets and reported solvency positions.[49] The problem resides not in volatility itself, but on the extent to which the reported solvency position may not accurately reflect economic fundamentals and the distortions that this may entail for the proper management of the insurance activity. In the presence of inaccurate reporting, markets may pressure insurers to expand their business or distribute profits, when reported solvency positions are artificially high, or alternatively, demand counter-productive restructuring, when the reported indicators are artificially low.

---

[48] For additional discussion on asset-liability management, please refer to the subsections above.

[49] As for interest-rate risk, in the standard formula, a smaller duration gap between assets and liabilities entails a smaller capital requirement for interest-rate risk (movements in the risk-free interest-rate term structure).

The contentious points just highlighted refer to the 2009 Framework Directive, which was undergoing a review at the point of drafting this report. The next sections consider in more detail the two aspects that are the core of this review, namely i) the distinction between spread (interest rate) risk and default (credit) risk and ii) the calibration of capital charges for long-term investing. Before considering these respects, Box 2 discusses the impact of capital charges on asset allocation, from a more general perspective.

Box 2. The influence of capital charges in Solvency II on asset allocation

Solvency II is not expected to bring insurers to seek re-capitalisation. The results of the fifth quantitative impact study (QIS 5) conducted by EIOPA (2011) indicate that less than 15% of insurers surveyed (2,520) would not meet the solvency capital requirement (SCR) while almost 50% had more than twice the required SCR. It follows that changes in asset allocation to meet the SCR are not generally needed (as far as these results will hold in the future, as the financial position of insurers is a moving target). However, the introduction of risk-sensitive capital charges creates an incentive to adjust asset allocation in favour of assets with lower charges, potentially irrespective of their broader suitability at the time and under those circumstances. The question for most insurers therefore is one of relative rather than absolute incentives. Figure 14 represents equivalent asset allocations under the standard formula; it illustrates the incentives embedded in the spread risk and equity risk sub-modules. Three observations should be noted: i) charges are higher for equity instruments, longer durations and lower-ratings; ii) covered bonds face lower charges than unsecured debt and iii) a zero risk weight applies to sovereign debt issued in the European Economic Area (EEA).

Figure 14. A stylised illustration of trade-offs between different asset classes

(Equivalent investment allocations under the Solvency II standard formula)

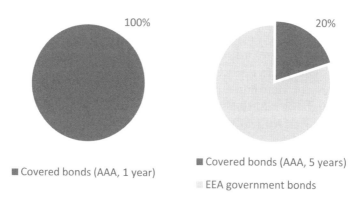

■ Covered bonds (AAA, 1 year)

■ Covered bonds (AAA, 5 years)

▨ EEA government bonds

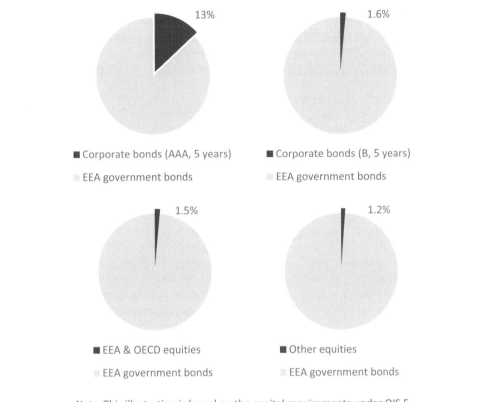

13%

1.6%

- ■ Corporate bonds (AAA, 5 years)
- ▨ EEA government bonds

- ■ Corporate bonds (B, 5 years)
- ▨ EEA government bonds

1.5%

1.2%

- ■ EEA & OECD equities
- ▨ EEA government bonds

- ■ Other equities
- ▨ EEA government bonds

Note: This illustration is based on the capital requirements under QIS 5.
It only considers capital charges from spread risk and equity risk.
Source: Committee on the Global Financial System (CGFS) (2011).

The incentives reflected above, which favour fixed income over equities, government bonds over corporate bonds, and short over long durations, are not as pronounced as they appear in the first instance, in view of:

- The relief provided for diversification, captured in a set of correlation matrices, which could reduce the effective risk charge applicable to equities by half (CGFS, 2011);
- The effect of public ratings, which should moderate the incentive to invest in sovereign bonds derived from zero risk-weights;
- The relief provided for longer durations by the matching adjustment (section 1.4) and the interest rate risk sub-module of the standard formula (EC, 2012a); and
- The benefits awarded for risk mitigation, hedging, reinsurance and securitisation.

Moreover, Solvency II allows insurers to develop and employ their own internal models (as an alternative to the standard formula, subject to supervisory approval) to calculate the SCR. The application of internal models could reduce capital requirements significantly – in QIS 5, the use of group internal models resulted in a reduction of the SCR by 20% on average. The extent to which insurers will develop internal models remains uncertain, however, due notably to the cost and complexity involved.

In sum, headline capital charges are not fully representative of the net effects of Solvency II on asset allocation. Moreover, solvency charges are but one of the factors influencing asset allocation, as presented in Table 5. In any event, the appropriate calibration of capital charges remains important.

Table 5. Selected factors influencing asset allocation

Regulatory-related	Market-related
◦ Solvency (capital) charges	◦ Relative returns offered by each asset class
◦ Available capital and discount rate for liabilities	◦ Volatility of each asset class
◦ Supervisory ladder (e.g. recovery periods)	◦ Ongoing business and legacy liabilities of each insurer
◦ Look-through to underlying investments	◦ Current business model and product mix of each insurer
◦ Internal models approved by supervisors	◦ Size of the balance sheet of each insurer
◦ Risk transfers (reinsurance, securitisation and derivatives)	◦ Expertise in less-liquid and alternative asset classes
◦ Benefits for diversification	◦ Public ratings (by rating agencies)

Source: Author.

Two studies on public ratings indicate that the effect of Solvency II capital charges may be more limited than sometimes portrayed: Höring (2012) finds, for an average European insurer, that gross market exposure would be lower under the rating model of S&P than under the Solvency II standard formula (nearly 25% lower). Yet, once diversification and adjustments are factored in, the SCR under S&P is nearly 68% higher than under Solvency II. Morgan Stanley (2013) however finds rating models to be less stringent for life insurers. However, looking at the SCR in this fashion fails to capture dynamic elements and makes results largely dependent on the model or average institution considered.

It is also widely acknowledged that the effective entry into force of Solvency II should not lead to shocks in capital markets, as it has been in the pipeline for over ten years and allows for transitional arrangements. No major relocations of assets are likely to occur. Some argue that such relocations have largely already taken place, in particular for equities, as a direct result of the introduction of mark-to-market accounting and risk-based supervision. Yet, the phenomenon is more accurately attributed to the convergence of several effects, including also market bubbles, the persistence of low returns and volatility, ageing populations in developed economies and higher awareness of the risks in the provision of guaranteed returns, leading to the general use of asset-liability management practices, relying on fixed-income investments (see McKinsey, 2011; CGFS, 2011; OECD, 2012).

Spread risk versus default risk...

Life insurers, given the certain and long-term profile of their liabilities, are able to hold assets to maturity or otherwise throughout their entire life cycle. When assets are held to maturity, as opposed to being available for trading, it is the default risk rather than the spread risk that matters. Prudential rules should appropriately distinguish between these different exposures.[50] The next few paragraphs address this question.

Credit risk or the risk of loss arising from fluctuations in the credit standing of an issuer or debtor, is usually understood to have two components: spread and default risk. The former is the risk of loss derived from a fluctuation in the level or volatility of the market price of a fixed-income instrument. It is defined in relative terms as the difference (or spread) between the quoted rate of return of the bond held (its market price) and the risk-free rate.

Within the balance sheet of an insurer or another institutional investor, spread risk is relevant for securities that may be subject to a forced sale, so as to meet an unforeseen liability cash-flow, or that are otherwise available for trading. By way of contrast, when a security is held to maturity, what matters is default risk, meaning the risk that an issuer will fail to honour its obligations to timely pay any agreed coupons or reimbursements of the principal.[51] It is hence the financial strength of the issuer or counterparty that determines default risk, rather than the volatility of asset prices in the marketplace.

When a fixed-income security is held to maturity, the investor bears primarily the risk of default and is largely unaffected by short-term volatility in the asset price, as s/he would not dispose of it before it matures. Holding assets to maturity (in particular fixed-income securities with long durations, matched to similarly long-term liabilities) is central to life insurance when it provides guarantees for long-term/retirement savings.[52] To ensure that those guarantees are honoured, an insurer would typically match liabilities against assets with a similar profile, in terms of duration and/or cash-flows. In so doing, it would mitigate the risk of forced sales and therefore the potential impact of spread risk in its portfolio.

---

[50] Article 105.5 of Solvency II distinguishes between: i) the risk of movements of the risk-free curve ('interest-rate risk'), ii) spread risk and iii) credit risk – regarding the calculation of the solvency capital requirement.

[51] Default risk also includes the costs related to the downgrading of ratings, for any of the assets held, including the costs linked to maintaining the credit quality of the investment portfolio.

[52] Article 132.2 of Solvency II requires that assets held to cover the technical provisions are "invested in a manner appropriate to the nature and duration of the insurance liabilities".

Asset-liability management (ALM) practices are therefore consequential in two respects: i) by cash-flow and duration matching, they increase the likelihood of meeting liabilities and ii) by holding assets to maturity, they expose investment portfolios to default risk rather than spread risk. Arguably the 2009 framework directive for Solvency II, however, did not take into account these two effects, which prompted its review under the Omnibus II Directive (still in the process of adoption at the time of drafting):

- *On the asset side of the balance sheet*, capital charges reflect a number of risks, including: i) interest rate risk or the sensitivity to changes in the yield curve or term structure of interest rates, ii) spread risk or the sensitivity to changes in credit spreads over the risk-free rates and iii) counterparty risk or the possible loss due to unexpected default of counterparties or debtors (Article 105). For assets held to maturity, it is argued that capital charges should not reflect interest-rate and spread risk but only default risk. The risks reflected in the charges applied to non-listed asset classes are called into question on similar grounds.

- *On the liability side of the balance sheet*, the term structure of the discount rates employed to calculate the present value of future liabilities is constructed on the basis of risk-free interest rates (the yield curve), since liabilities are hard promises. Utilising a higher rate or discount, that is, assuming a higher rate of return on assets and a lower present value of liabilities, would go against the principle of prudent valuations, since it is uncertain that a higher rate of return can be earned. However, where liabilities are matched to assets with a similar duration and cash-flow profile and assets are held to maturity, it is argued that the discount rate should reflect the effects of this matching.

In order to capture the actual risks to which life insurers and beneficiaries are effectively exposed, it is important to reflect the economic fundamentals derived from asset-liability matching. It matters both to support best practices in the operation of life insurance and to ensure market participants get an accurate picture of the solvency position of an insurer by looking at reported figures. As a corollary, it should also reduce volatility in the reported solvency position of insurers, since fluctuations in spreads would only be fed into balance sheets to the extent they are indicative of changes in default risk.

Volatility in own funds and reported solvency ratios is not a problem in itself but only when it does not accurately reflect actual solvency. It may then lead to unintended effects such as heightened pressures to distribute profits or compete aggressively, when reported solvency would be high (under low spreads). Or pressure to pursue detrimental restructuring if reported solvency falls below supervisory thresholds (under high spreads). While such extreme scenarios are likely to be rare, their impact should not be underestimated.

To limit artificial volatility and better capture the risk mitigation effect of asset-liability management, a matching adjustment (MA) was proposed during the Omnibus II review of the 2009 Solvency II Directive.[53] The proposed MA would be applied to the discount rate for eligible liabilities and be equal to the spread over the risk-free rate on admissible backing assets, less an estimate of the costs of default (EIOPA, 2013d). In this manner, it would adjust the discounted value of eligible liabilities to the risks effectively borne in the investment portfolio: eligible liabilities are discounted at the rate of return of eligible backing assets, by projecting their future contractual cash-flows (principal and coupon) minus an estimation of the reduction in contractual cash-flows arising from expected defaults or downgrades. Figure 15 presents this process graphically.

Figure 15. Stylised representation of the matching adjustment process

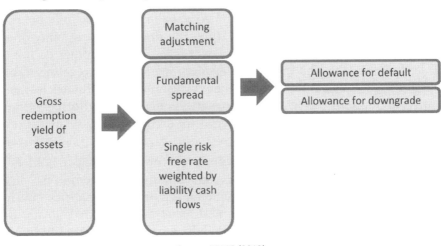

Source: KPMG (2012).

---

[53] The matching adjustment (MA) is part of a broader set of measures aimed at limiting the impact of artificial volatility on the provision of certain insurance products, in particular long-term guarantees (European Commission, 2012e; EIOPA, 2013c). Under this 'Long-Term Guarantee Assessment' (LTGA) and following the terms of reference agreed on 14 December 2012 by the European Council, Parliament and Commission (in legislative trialogue), EIOPA evaluated five versions of the matching adjustment, the application of a counter-cyclical premium to the relevant risk-free interest rate term structure, the extension of the recovery period, extrapolation and transitional measures. The findings of EIOPA were presented on 14 June 2013 (EIOPA, 2013g).

The application of a matching adjustment, while desirable to increase the accuracy of reported solvency and avoid hindering the provision of long-term guarantees unduly, raises however a number of practical concerns:

○ *Identifying default risk, separating it from spread risk*

There is evidence that movements in bond spreads are not driven by default risk alone but also by relative liquidity and other non-credit related factors. For any spread, however, separating the share explained by default risk from other components is not a straightforward task.[54] Under the proposed MA, this 'fundamental spread' would be calculated independently by the insurer for each portfolio, which springs naturally from the purpose of the MA but nevertheless poses a supervisory challenge.

○ *Determining eligible liabilities and admissible assets*

Assets may only be matched against liabilities that are certain as regards the volume and timing of payments. In theory, liabilities can be fully defined in both respects. In practice, however, typically due to the possibility of early redemptions or the coverage of longevity risk, liability profiles do not tend to be fully certain. The insurance business works by aggregating multiple liabilities (policies) and modelling them by estimating contingencies such as early redemptions, unpaid premiums and life expectancy for beneficiaries. The question, for the MA, is the degree of certainty in the liability profile that would warrant its application.

A narrow application of the MA would only operate if policy-holders had no other options (no ability to stop contributions or redeem early) and no guarantee was offered upon death. Some accumulation policies offering a guaranteed return at a given date and some annuities that do not cover longevity risk are good examples. While a broader MA would apply to other products but only to the share of the liabilities deemed to be certain (total liabilities less estimated contingencies). The matter is ultimately one of supervisory comfort with internal modelling of liabilities by insurers for the purposes of regulatory compliance.

As for admissible assets, while strictly speaking only fixed-income securities can be matched, two questions remain: the minimum credit quality required (if any) and the extent to which other instruments may be admitted. The MA should not provide an incentive to invest in poor-quality assets but should probably not confine itself to the highest-graded assets either, which

---

[54] See Giesecke et al. (2010), Webber & Churm (2007), Manning (2004) and related commentary by Towers Watson (2012).

could limit useful investments in the real economy.[55] At the same time, extending the application of the MA to other asset classes could facilitate some forms of long-term investing. In this respect, the MA could be extended to include alternative assets with bond-like cash-flows, such as infrastructure debt – it should be noted that a replication portfolio based on illiquid assets would typically be less expensive than one based on perfectly liquid ones (Gründl, 2013). Furthermore, the principles behind the MA could in theory also be applied to, for instance, dividends from equities or rents from real estate, by applying a prudential factor to expected cash-flows.

○ *Controlling for reinvestment and counterparty risks.*

Partial matching results in reinvestment risk, which can be defined broadly as the risk that future market rates would be below the return guaranteed to policy-holders. Perfect matching against assets with identical durations and cash-flows is rarely feasible in practice, particularly for very long maturities. The question is how to combine the application of the MA with a suitable reflection of reinvestment risk, in case of imperfect matching, where assets may be held to maturity but would mature before the last cash-flows of the liabilities they back. Developing a methodology for this purpose is unlikely to be a straightforward exercise (Towers Watson, 2013).

The MA framework would also need to control for the potential increase in counterparty risk indirectly derived from its application. If perfect matching is required and the use of derivatives and hedging practices is (inevitably) allowed to achieve identical durations and cash-flows, the counterparty risk borne by insurers would increase. While this additional (and to some extent regulatory-induced) counterparty risk would be taken into account by the capital charges for the instruments concerned, it still raises wider prudential concerns for insurers and the stability of the financial system (CGFS, 2011).

○ *Aligning it to best practices in asset-liability management*

Good asset-liability management requires frequent rebalancing of matched portfolios, as the term structure of interest rate tends not to move in parallel

---

[55] The benefits of the MA from a reporting and compliance perspective could encourage investments in lower-rated assets. This development could prompt the introduction of requirements regarding the minimum credit quality of admissible assets (it should however be acknowledged that, following the 2008 financial crisis and the ongoing sovereign debt crisis, top-rated assets have become relatively scarce). While the credit quality of assets is already taken into account in the capital charges (under the standard formula to calculate the SCR), lower quality is usually explained by a higher risk of default, which should be captured in the application of the MA.

but to become flatter or steeper, leading to maturity mismatches.[56] Rating downgrades for assets backing liabilities would also invite rebalancing. In both these instances the applicability of the MA would be altered. However, given a large portfolio, it will typically be more efficient to reallocate some assets to back other liabilities or even to sell some assets to purchase others. To the extent that such rebalancing is economically efficient, it should be recognised in the application of the MA. The instances in which rebalancing is possible may however need to be limited in order to prevent insurers from behaving strategically i.e. to optimise reported solvency rather than to better manage risks and portfolios.

○ *Deciding the best reporting for its effects*

The risk mitigation effects of asset-liability matching, measured by the MA, can be reported in a number of formats, including as a separate entry on the balance sheet or integrated in another balance sheet value. In the interest of transparency, the impact of the MA should be disaggregated and publicly disclosed. The MA should therefore appear as additional information for all stakeholders to best assess the solvency position and business of an insurer.

To conclude, it is important to note that recognising the effect of ALM practices (cash-flow and duration matching) is important, not only to better reflect the risks effectively run in life insurance, but also to support long-term investing. In effect, matching long-term liabilities with long-term assets, held to maturity, provides a source of long-term and stable funding for issuers. While the ability of insurers to concentrate on default risk rather than spread risk should lead to a deeper focus on value fundamentals rather than short-term price movements. In the context of long-term investing, the European Commission (2012a) asked EIOPA to calibrate capital charges for some assets, as discussed below.

Calibration of capital charges...

The European Commission (2012a) asked EIOPA to calibrate capital charges in the Solvency II standard formula for infrastructure financing, SME financing, socially responsible investments and social business financing – through debt, equity and structured finance, including securitisation and project bonds.

As an exercise to closely assess the risks linked to alternative investments, such as venture capital or infrastructure, it should increase understanding among regulators and supervisors. But the relative scarcity of performance and risk data make it difficult to build a distinct capital charge for each asset class – and if no such charge is found, the one for equities applies. Assessing the risks for

---

[56] For a discussion on rebalancing, see the subsections above.

each asset class separately should lead to a more accurate reflection of risks (from an historical perspective). But it may or may not bring about charges that are lower than the ones applicable to equities, as the specific risk for the given asset class may be found to be higher. In a preliminary assessment, EIOPA (2013d) did not find enough supporting evidence to arrive at distinct charges. The discussion remains however open, in the search for alternative methodologies better suited to assess risks in less-liquid asset classes. This calibration is not a one-off exercise but could be reviewed periodically (according to the Omnibus II proposal[57]).

As a cautionary note, it is worth recalling that 'long-term investing' (defined as investment conducive to gross capital formation) is not among the objectives pursued by Solvency II, as it bears no weight on the interest of policy-holders and beneficiaries. The promotion of gross capital formation may however have overall positive effects in an economy and therefore also on beneficiaries and insurance undertakings, albeit through this indirect channel.

In sum...

This section has discussed institutional long-term investing today, focusing on the provision of guaranteed returns, the interest of beneficiaries and the impact of changes in macroeconomic conditions and business models. It also considered the role of regulation and the ongoing reform of the prudential framework for insurers and pension funds in Europe.

The ability of life insurers and pension schemes to invest long-term is given, in the first instance, by the long-term horizons inherent in saving for retirement. But it also depends on the characteristics of the product or scheme operated. And it is affected by prudential and other considerations embedded in the regulatory framework.

Products and schemes incorporating guarantees play a useful social function as they increase pension safety and help mitigate income inequality at retirement. The provision of guarantees requires specific investment practices, known as asset-liability management (ALM) based on the matching of liabilities against fixed-income instruments with similar duration and cash-flows. Under long-term investment horizons, these practices are inherently conducive to long-term investing as assets with long life-cycles are held over long periods of time or to maturity, providing long-term and stable funding to issuers.

Retirement solutions that incorporate no (or limited) guarantees are also able to invest long-term, as long as redemption policies are sufficiently illiquid.

---

[57] Proposal for a Directive amending Directives 2003/71/EC and 2009/138/EC [COM(2011) 8 final]

They may also allocate a higher share of their assets to equity and equity-like instruments, and less-liquid asset classes if the size of the scheme allows. Long-term investment horizons under restricted liquidity towards investors and large-sized funds should lead to more patient, engaged and productive capital being deployed in the economy.

Persistently low-interest rates reduce the ability to deliver guaranteed returns above inflation and call for hybrid solutions that combine pension safety with potentially higher adequacy. They also put pressure on the solvency position of providers having to service high legacy liabilities and demand more careful supervision, within an appropriate regulatory framework.

Solvency II is central to improving the regulation and supervision of insurance and is leading the process towards greater sophistication in risk management and investment practices. It should, however, duly calibrate capital charges and recognise the risk mitigation effects derived from ALM practices, as envisaged under the matching adjustment (MA), whose role and trade-offs this section considered in detail. The conclusion from this exercise could then be used to help inform the debate surrounding the extension of risk-based supervision to the provision of guarantees by pension funds (section 2.2).

2. THE SINGLE MARKET FOR LONG-TERM SAVINGS

The single market potential remains largely unexplored where it comes to long-term investing and retirement saving solutions, broadly accessible to households in Europe. This chapter considers less-liquid investment funds, occupational pensions and direct retail investments, from an EU single market perspective, in view of their importance to channel retail savings with a long-term horizon towards adequate investment opportunities. It also considers the current EU framework for investor protection, and ways in which it could be optimised to foster retail access to long-term investing and retirement solutions – while improving protection.

2.1 A single market for less-liquid funds

The EU regulatory framework for retail investment funds favours liquidity towards investors (in terms of redemptions) to the detriment of investments in less-liquid assets. As EU-regulated retail funds, UCITS (undertakings for collective investment in transferable securities) are required to repurchase or redeem their units at the request of any unit holder.[58] Hence, UCITS are not allowed to invest directly in less-liquid asset classes. Yet, in several member states, there are regulatory frameworks that allow retail investors to access less-liquid assets in a fund format with limited redemptions (EC, 2013d).

The adoption of the AIFMD (alternative investment fund managers Directive) in 2011 facilitated the introduction of sector-specific and narrow product rules for investment funds, in addition to UCITS.[59] Indeed, European venture capital funds (EuVECAs) and social entrepreneurship funds (EuSEFs) were adopted shortly after the introduction of the Directive.[60] The AIFMD embodies the basic regulatory framework for fund management in Europe – management rules for

---

[58] Article 84, Directive 2009/65/EC.

[59] Directive 2011/61/EU.

[60] Regulation 345/2013 and Regulation 346/2013. The regulatory frameworks for EuVECAs and EuSEFs build upon the AIFMD, although they apply when assets under management do not exceed the *de minimis* threshold in Article 3.2.b of the AIFMD.

UCITS remain formally separate, despite converging in substance (de Manuel & Lannoo, 2012).[61]

As a matter of fostering investor choice and facilitating long-term investing, a pan-European framework for less-liquid investment funds has been advocated by industry, regulators and experts.[62] In building such a framework however, a number of hurdles are present, including: i) aligning redemption profiles with underlying liquidity, ii) addressing valuation difficulties and related problems arising from the illiquidity of the underlying and iii) responding to insufficient awareness among some investors, as well as mitigating the risk of mismanaged expectations.

The difficulties experienced by some funds invested in less-liquid asset classes to meet redemptions before and during the 2008 financial crisis illustrated the importance of aligning redemption policies with the liquidity of underlying assets. The example of retail OEREFs (open-end real estate funds), popular in Germany but regulated in at least other nine member states, prompted national authorities to introduce lock-in periods and advance notice requirements.[63] The substantial liquidity transformation performed by OEREFs resulted in liquidity crisis in some funds, which stranded investors and lea to sizeable economic and confidence losses (Bannier et al., 2007).

---

[61] The UCITS Directive comprises both management rules (as the AIFMD) and product rules (in contrast with the AIFMD). With respect to management rules, the proposal to amend Directive 2009/65/EC [COM (2012) 350] will further align the UCITS Directive with the AIFMD, regarding in particular the depositary function. In addition, a 2012 consultation on UCITS, product rules, liquidity management, depositary, money market funds and long-term investments is also expected to lead to further alignment of the UCITS framework with some of the provisions in the AIFMD (EC, 2012g).

[62] Examples of support to less-liquid fund are: *"54% of respondents felt that a common EU framework dedicated to long-term investments for retail investors is needed* » Industry survey on long-term savings (EFAMA, 2012) « *Key action 6: Boost long-term investment in the real economy by facilitating access to long-term investment funds"* Single Market Act II (EC, 2012h). *"A new long-term vehicle for retail investors should be introduced in Europe: Retail investors would benefit from having access to relatively illiquid asset classes to channel part of their long-term savings, including part of their retirement savings. A harmonised regulatory framework for long-term retail funds (LTRFs) should therefore be considered."* Rethinking Asset Management (de Manuel & Lannoo, 2012).

[63] For instance, the Investor Protection and Functionality Improvement Act of 11 February 2011, imposes a 12-month notice period for redemptions, applicable to existing and new investors, and a 24-month holding period for new investors in OEREFs regulated in Germany. This same Act also prescribes stricter leverage limits and valuation requirements. Additional restrictions are envisaged by the German Government as part of the transposition of the AIFMD (European Commission, 2013d).

Article 16 of the AIFMD requires managers to ensure, for every fund, that the liquidity profile of the underlying investments and redemption policy of fund units are consistent. Managers need to have liquidity management procedures in place and regularly conduct stress tests. Funds also need to devise a specific redemption policy for exceptional market circumstances and communicate it to investors, in principle professional clients, ex-ante (Article 23).

The provisions in the AIFMD strive to incorporate the lessons learned during the financial crisis regarding the inhibiting effects of unaccounted maturity and liquidity transformation for investors individually and the financial system as a whole (Turner, 2009; De Larosière et al., 2009). It follows that any framework for investment funds biased towards less-liquid underlying assets would need to incorporate clear limits on redemptions and avoid giving a false impression of liquidity to inexperienced investors.[64]

While illiquidity deters some investors from accessing investment funds, there are several examples (at national level) of fund frameworks that impose severe restrictions on redemptions and, yet, have found relative success among retail investors. The European Commission (2013c) reports that 70% of assets under management by closed-end funds in Germany originate from retail investors directly. In the same vein, 30% of the money raised by private equity funds in France originated from retail investors, between 2008 and the first half of 2012.[65] While the market for less-liquid investment funds may be relatively modest in size, when compared to UCITS, investor demand exists and could grow in the future.

In other member states, retail access to less-liquid investment funds is difficult and is coupled with insufficient awareness among retail investors about long-term investing. As a first step, to enable retail access, a harmonised framework would be needed; including product structuring and investor protection rules. In a survey of industry participants conducted by EFAMA (2012), a majority of respondents agreed that a common EU framework for long-term investments for retail investors is needed. Such a framework would facilitate awareness but additional awareness-raising initiatives would be needed. In this same survey, a majority of respondents also saw merit in a common information initiative on long-term savings.

In devising a pan-European framework for retail funds invested in less-liquid asset classes, the question revolves around the definition of eligible assets and diversification thresholds. Once the importance of aligning redemption policies

---

[64] Liquidity, however, is a continuum that allows for intermediate solutions (for instance, from daily, weekly, monthly, quarterly liquidity and above). See section 1.2.

[65] Tax incentives are thought to support these figures.

with the liquidity of the underlying is acknowledged, it becomes apparent that two alternative designs are possible: i) funds fully invested in less-liquid assets, redeemable only upon maturity, or ii) funds partially invested in liquid assets, where intermediary redemptions would be possible at given intervals under certain conditions, notably advance notice. The latter funds would therefore need to incorporate a liquidity management function.

Each category of funds, however, may serve a different purpose: i) an illiquid or closed-end fund for investors able and willing to commit their capital over a given period of time, in contrast with ii) a balanced fund, for those investors interested rather in gaining a diversified exposure both to liquid and less-liquid asset classes – and willing to accept some restrictions on redemptions. The first model would maximise the exposure to the illiquidity premium but, precisely due to its illiquidity, may be more difficult for some investors to access – while the second model would give only partial exposure to the illiquidity premium but may be more broadly accessible. One model does not however exclude the other and, in fact, both are complementary and needed to complete the choice afforded to retail investors in Europe, beyond the high liquidity in transferable securities offered by UCITS.[66] However, beyond less-liquid asset classes, long-term investing also takes the form of low turnover and strategic equity stakes and investments in fixed-income securities with long maturities. Such practices would also necessitate redemption restrictions and may more easily find their place within a framework for balanced funds.

---

[66] It has also been proposed that the so-called 'trash ratio' in UCITS (10% of assets under management – Article 50.2.a Directive 2009/65/EC) could be allowed to incorporate less-liquid asset classes. However, holdings of such assets would alter the liquidity profile of UCITS and sit uncomfortably with daily redemptions, heightening the risk derived from maturity and liquidity transformation (defined for an investment fund by the misalignment between the liquidity of its underlying and that of its units or shares). Certain less-liquid asset classes are accessible by UCITS using derivative financial instruments, subject to conditions (for a summary, see ESMA 2012/832). In a derivative transaction, the liquidity of the underlying is, in a way, substituted by the liquidity of the counterparty and, hence, counterparty exposure limits and collateral management requirements are put in place. The use of derivatives to access less-liquid asset classes in UCITS is linked to regulatory restrictions (or permissiveness, depending on the perspective). Yet, more widely, the use of derivatives to access less-liquid assets is also explained by typically lower transaction costs, in comparison to direct access (de Manuel & Lannoo, 2012).

Box 3. The proposal on European long-term investment funds

In June 2013, the European Commission tabled a legislative initiative (2013/0214 COD) containing product rules on closed-end funds, invested in less-liquid asset classes and open to retail investors, under the denomination ELTIFs (European long-term investment funds). The proposal, in the form of a regulation, directly applicable in all member states, builds on the AIFMD framework for managers, and follows a period of extensive analysis, review of regimes at national level and consultation with stakeholders (EC, 2013c).

ELTIFs would invest at least 70% of their capital in less-liquid assets and comply with strict diversification requirements – not to invest more than 10% of their capital in any single individual real asset or eligible undertaking (below). The remainder 30% of capital may be invested in liquid financial instruments (UCITS eligible assets) but no more than 5% in any single issuer (Article 12).

ELTIFs would acquire assets directly from qualifying portfolio undertakings (non-financial and non-traded) or take direct participation in projects. Investments may take the form of equity participations, debt instruments, loans, or the direct holding of individual assets requiring an up-front capital expenditure of at least €10 million. They may also invest in other ELTIFs, and regulated venture capital funds (EuVECAs) and social entrepreneurship funds (EuSEFs) (Articles 9 and 10).

ELTIFs would be prohibited from short-selling assets, gaining exposure to commodities, entering into any arrangement that may encumber its assets and using derivatives, except for certain hedging purposes (Article 8). Leverage is hence restricted, as is the borrowing of cash (Article 14).

ELTIFs would be closed-end funds, meaning redemptions are not possible before the end of the life of the fund, which must be a specific date, decided by the manager ex-ante and disclosed to investors before they enter the fund. The life of the ELTIF should be long enough to cover the life-cycle of each individual asset (Article 16). Units may be traded however on a secondary market (Article 17) – although such trading should not lead to a false impression of liquidity, as a significant discount tends to be involved and liquidity is volatile in these markets.

The product structuring rules above are accompanied by requirements on disclosure and transparency, regarding both costs and the illiquid nature of the fund (Articles 21 and 22). If marketed to retail investors, additional requirements would apply, including a right of withdrawal for 14 days after the subscription of units from the fund (Article 24).

The European Commission anticipates two demand cohorts for ELTIFs: i) retail investors and ii) small institutional investors, with assets from €100 million to €1.5 billion – for which pooled vehicles are the most economically efficient way to access less-liquid asset classes, and a regulated fund format is expected to ease due diligence and facilitate investments. ELTIFs can also play a pivotal role in structuring defined-contribution personal pension solutions (chapter 3).

Box 4. Is there space for retail balanced funds with a long-term orientation in Europe?

Retail balanced funds in Europe could help broaden access to less-liquid asset classes and facilitate long-term investment practices, such as low-turnover equity strategies, strategic equity stakes and investments in fixed-income instruments with long maturities. 'Buy and hold' strategies can be implemented within the UCITS framework but are limited by the high liquidity offered towards investors. While the stability of assets under management (in terms of volume) facilitates long-term practices in some UCITS, the lack of restrictions on redemptions ultimately imposes a heightened duty on managers to ensure liquidity. In addition, daily valuations, short-term risk metrics and the use of relative benchmarks to evaluate performance and remuneration do not facilitate long-term investing either.

A framework for balanced funds could be aligned with long-term investing by presenting: i) limited redemption windows and advance notice requirements, in line with the lower liquidity embedded in long-term investing practices and certain asset classes; ii) absolute return targets, based on fundamental macroeconomic or sector-specific variables rather than peer short-term performance; and iii) clear messages to investors about the medium- to long-term nature of the investment vehicle, helping to align incentives with managers. At the same time, by still providing some opportunity for redemptions, the proposed model of balanced funds may gather success within a broad investor base.

The proposed retail balanced funds would invest in both UCITS-eligible and ELTIF-eligible assets. ELTIF assets (equity participations, debt instruments or loans in non-financial non-traded undertakings and direct holdings of individual assets) would account for at least 10% and a maximum of 30% of assets under management – this range could be narrowed down further to the benefit of standardisation. The funds would be able to access less-liquid assets directly or via participations in ELTIFs, EuVECAs or EuSEFs.

Long-term balanced funds would be driven by absolute return targets in line with their investment horizons. And they would publish their own policy regarding the application of long-term and responsible investing criteria to their investment practices. The use of derivative instruments would be limited to an exhaustive list of hedging purposes. Leverage would also be clearly limited, as a share of assets under management, following a commitment approach.

Redemption policies would need to be aligned with the share of ELTIF assets targeted by the fund in its instruments of incorporation, and its policy on long-term investing in liquid assets. Investors would need to be duly informed of the long-term nature of these funds and their redemption policies, both in normal and adverse market circumstances. If adverse market conditions severely impact the ability of the fund to meet redemptions, investors should be made aware ex-ante that the fund may become partially illiquid, for the share of ELTIF assets, until the end of their life-cycle is attained. Equal treatment to all investors should be ensured in such instances, including by segregating ELTIF assets and providing participations by way of redemptions.

Balanced funds are thought to be an adequate default solution for defined-contribution pensions (chapter 3). Within a pan-European framework for personal pensions, balanced funds (with a long-term orientation, as described in this box) could provide an efficient mechanism for the delivery of adequate retirement income – as far as it is coupled with an appropriate market structure. Chapter 3 considers these aspects in detail, including the merits and drawbacks of balanced funds as default solutions.

Box 5. An accompanying market structure for balanced funds

Higher standardisation in the market for investments funds could attract investors who would otherwise not consider this market by: i) mitigating the complexity and burden of choice, ii) raising visibility versus the use of traditional bank deposits for saving purposes and iii) helping to focus competition among providers on solution quality and costs over product proliferation and marketing. A simple and standardised marketplace for balanced funds could therefore benefit both investors – as far as cost efficiencies would be realised and passed on to them, thanks to a competitive market setting – and industry – as far as it would reach investors previously deterred by the complexity of the market setting and multiplicity of choice. It would also benefit the economy, as it would help channel available long-term financing towards long-term investing needs, in a transparent setting limiting maturity transformation and hence related risks to financial stability.

Box 4 (above) advances general principles that could guide the design of a pan-European framework for balanced funds. Such funds could be a potential alternative to traditional bank deposits (for deposits held with a long-term purpose and for individuals willing to accept explicit market risk) or very liquid investment funds. An accompanying market structure policy would be instrumental for maximising efficiencies in the industrial setting, accessibility and ultimately value for investors. It is proposed that a narrow playing field for competition would be laid out, limiting the offer of balanced funds to one product per originator – asset manager, insurer or other qualifying undertaking (each fund would be named 'Balanced Fund' followed by the name of the provider). It is also proposed that a pan-European processing architecture would be established, including a single clearing house, to ensure that a genuine single market develops, fostering optimal fund size and cost structures. In addition a single online information tool could be devised to provide general information about balanced funds and help investors compare among the different providers of this standardised investment solution. These aspects are more closely considered in chapter 3, from the perspective of a pan-European framework for personal pensions.

2.2 A single market for occupational pensions

Pensions linked to employment relationships carry different weights in national pension systems. In the majority of member states where occupational schemes play a prominent role, guaranteed benefits are still dominant (EIOPA, 2012c). Yet, the transition towards limited and conditional guarantees and towards hybrid and defined contribution arrangements is in progress and expected to intensify – section 1.4 considers the reasons behind this transition. Given their funded status, occupational schemes have both the purpose and liability profile/return targets that enable long-term investing.[67]

In 2003, a Directive on institutions for occupational retirement provision (IORP) was introduced as a first step to build a single market for funded occupational pension funds operating mainly defined benefit and hybrid arrangements.[68] Defined contribution schemes are only partially in scope, while some defined benefit and hybrid solutions are entirely excluded from the directive – notably book reserve schemes, where liabilities are accounted for in the balance sheet of the employer. Figure 16 presents the share of assets in the occupational pension sector that is subject to the IORP Directive.

Figure 16. Assets of IORPs as % of assets of occupational pension sector

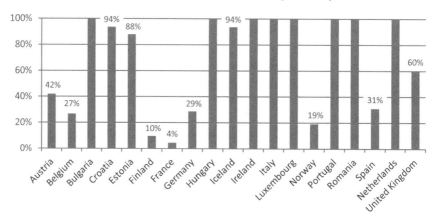

Source: Pensions Europe. Data for 2010.

The 2003 IORP Directive, based on minimum harmonisation, had an 'enabling' purpose for the cross-border provision of occupational pensions – that is, when the sponsor and the IORP are located in a different member state – and (more indirectly) the pooling of schemes by companies operating in more than one member state. The Directive distinguishes between prudential supervision of the *home member state* – the state where the IORP is located – and social and labour law (SLL) of the *host member state* – where beneficiaries are or have been employed.[69]

---

[67] Defined contribution pension solutions lack formal liabilities (no returns are guaranteed) but may be designed and managed to achieve absolute long-term return targets, under limited liquidity to investors (in terms of redemptions).

[68] Directive 2003/41/EC.

[69] Articles 6.i, 6.j and 20, Directive 2003/41/EC.

In addition, the Directive pursues higher sophistication in the management of occupational pension funds across the European Union, within a single market that would spur convergence towards best practices from advanced member states. It also seeks better supervision in the interest of current and future beneficiaries, market efficiency and financial stability. The Union is otherwise limited in its ambition to promote occupational pensions by the allocation of competences in this area in favour of member states.[70]

Regarding the objective of enabling cross-border arrangements, the Directive has achieved little success so far. In 2012, there were only 84 cross-border IORPs out of roughly 120,000 such schemes in Europe (EIOPA, 2012d; European Commission, 2012e). The heightened compliance burden affecting cross-border operations and the lack of clarity in the division of competences between home and host member states is thought to deter sponsors from such operations (European Commission, 2011a). Removing these barriers would be instrumental to enabling the single market and its associated efficiencies, cost savings and diversification benefits. There is scope for further clarification of what constitutes cross-border activity and which criteria belong to social and labour law versus prudential law/supervision (EIOPA, 2010 and 2012d; European Commission, 2010a and 2011a).

As regards prudential supervision, the 2003 IORP Directive relied foremost on mutual recognition. It only set general principles affecting technical provisions and their funding, own funds, investments, and management and custody.[71] It requires the calculation of technical provisions to be certified by an actuary and gives member states discretion regarding discount rates for liabilities. Funding should be sufficient at all times or otherwise a recovery plan would be adopted. And the 'prudent person' principle should guide investments, with limits to the ability of member states to restrict eligible assets.

Member states have interpreted and implemented the general principles above in diverse ways, which makes mutual recognition difficult in practice[72] and can induce harmful competition among jurisdictions.[73] At the same time, IORPs are

---

[70] Articles 4.2.b and 21.3 (requiring unanimity at Council level for adopting measures concerning social security or social protection) of the Treaty on the Functioning of the European Union.

[71] Articles 15 and 16, 17, 18, and 19, respectively, Directive 2003/41/EC.

[72] "Belgium: Cross-border Barriers – What lessons can be learned from the failure of French UMR to establish an IORP domiciled in Belgium", Investments and Pension Europe, March 2013 (www.ipe.com/magazine/belgium-cross-border-barriers_50273.php).

[73] The lack of harmonised prudential standards is an incentive for regulatory and supervisory competition among potential fund domiciles, which may come at the expense of investor protection and financial stability.

significant operators in financial markets. Their size exceeds €2,900 billion in terms of assets under management, that is, around 25% of GDP for the EU altogether – but in some member states assets in occupational pensions exceed GDP by a multiple. Hence, going forward, minimum harmonisation becomes difficult to justify, in light of the potential externalities and the lessons learned during the financial crisis (Turner, 2009; De Larosière et al., 2009).[74]

The European Commission communicated in May 2013 that it would present a legislative proposal revising the IORP Directive in autumn 2013.[75] The proposal will be limited to governance and supervision (pillar 2) and transparency and disclosure (pillar 3). The Commission envisages tabling a revision of solvency requirements (pillar 1) at a later stage, once the necessary quantitative impact assessments would be concluded (EIOPA, 2013b). The diversity of occupational pension systems across member states makes the harmonisation of quantitative requirements difficult in practice (section 1.4).

In the interest of beneficiaries and long-term investing, it is however important to strengthen the quality and accessibility of occupational pensions in Europe. The single market can indeed deliver efficiencies and innovation, cost savings (higher net returns) and diversification benefits – including eased access to less-liquid asset classes. But in reforming the IORP Directive, a distinction should be made between: i) dealing with legacy issues versus prospectively devising a framework for occupational pensions in Europe and ii) a common supervisory framework versus the values of parameters in the framework. The revision of IORP would benefit from a holistic approach, to foster employer participation in pension arrangements and long-term investing practices across the spectrum of defined benefit, hybrid and defined contribution schemes.

○ *Dealing with legacy final salary schemes and instances of severe underfunding.* As traditional defined benefit schemes close to new members and occupational pensions move towards hybrid and pure defined contribution, authorities should separate legacy problems from the design of a framework catering for the future of funded pensions in Europe. In dealing with cases of severe underfunding, coordination at EU level would be necessary in any instances at risk of generating negative externalities for other member states, in view of their size or significance. Yet, member states should keep some discretion

---

[74] The European Union is also constrained to ensure appropriate regulation and supervision of pension funds in all member states, given its Treaty mandate and following the G20 consensus on subjecting all areas of financial intermediation to appropriate regulation and supervision (London, April 2009).

[75] MEMO/13/454 of 23 May 2013.

to decide the specific timing and fashion of intervention, particularly where their fiscal capacity is at stake.

○ *Providing a platform for hybrid arrangements and innovation in solution design.* A prospective EU framework for occupational pensions should not be limited to addressing prudential concerns in traditional defined benefit schemes. It should instead provide *"a continuum of regulation that allows pension schemes to be created – and properly regulated – at any point on the risk-sharing spectrum"* (NAPF, 2012). Quantitative requirements, where applicable, should hence be fully reflective of the characteristics of the pension contract and the distribution of risks among sponsor, participants and any other stakeholder (section 1.4). Qualitative requirements – in particular, governance and communications – should be afforded greater attention, as schemes move away from defined benefit, to ensure adequate alignment of defined contribution solutions with retirement goals and long-term investing (chapter 3).

○ *Facilitating solutions able to follow individuals.* During their career, individuals move across an increasing number of positions and employers. They would therefore benefit from pension solutions that follow them from one job to another, while permitting the participation of employers in their funding. This result is achieved via facilitating the transferability of accumulated savings or via meta-schemes, covering a whole industry sector or the entire working population.[76] Such solutions allow for: i) costs savings, given scale economies, ii) diversification benefits, including eased access to less-liquid assets and iii) more conscious asset allocation, as assets are not scattered across multiple pots (chapter 3).[77]

○ *Promoting scale to minimise costs and maximise the long-term investing potential.* The dispersion of operating costs for funded pensions across member states indicates that the single market can have positive effects by fostering higher scale and integration. Countries with large numbers of small funds tend to have higher operating costs on average than countries with a small number of relatively large funds (OECD, 2011c, Figure 17). In addition, scale is directly related to the ability to access less-liquid asset classes, given the

---

[76] Examples are industry schemes in the Netherlands (covering workers in a given industry sector, in accordance with collective bargaining agreements), ATP in Denmark or NEST in the UK.

[77] Chapter 3 explores personal pensions (which could also allow for the participation of employers in their funding) and the alignment of incentives in defined contribution and hybrid schemes with long-term investing and retirement goals.

expertise needed and the sizeable minimum investments typically required (section 1.1 and chapter 3).

Figure 17. Operating costs for private pensions in selected countries

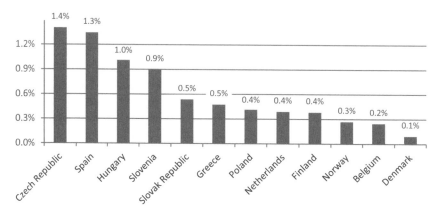

Source: OECD (2011c). Data for 2010. Share of total assets.
Includes investment expenses and administrative costs.

2.3 A single market for investor protection

Confidence and trust in investment products and services are central to driving investment flows, operating as a pre-condition to the accumulation of savings. In the context of long-term and retirement savings, retail investor protection is of particular relevance, given notably: i) the cumulative impact of costs and fees on net returns, which is more severe the longer the investment horizon,[78] ii) the growing significance of long-term investment decisions for the future income security of individuals, as governments and employers reduce benefits and shift risks and iii) the cognitive limitations and behavioural biases affecting individuals when they deal with long-term and retirement savings – including procrastination, difficulties to understand compounding and irrational reactions to short-term volatility and perceived loss[79] (Charter et al.,

---

[78] Section 3.1 illustrates with examples the impact on net returns of what may appear to a retail investor as a very small yearly fee, and how this impact increases with the investment horizon.

[79] In an experiment conducted in the UK by NEST (national employment savings trust) to better understand reactions to volatility and loss, participating individuals were explained the functioning of defined contribution schemes and were later confronted with short-term volatility in accumulated values. Individuals expressed emotions such as feeling cheated, robbed or misled and looked for someone to blame or punish (Horack et al., 2010a). These emotions led to irrational forms of behaviour, such as stopping contributions.

2010; Horack et al., 2010; De Meza et al., 2008). The European framework for investor protection needs to take due account of these issues, in building a single market that fosters accessibility to long-term investing and retirement solutions.

A simple taxonomy of policy tools for investor protection would distinguish: i) *know your product rules* – product structuring rules and suitability requirements at the structuring stage, ii) *disclosure requirements* – pre-contractual and ongoing disclosure standards, iii) *know your customer rules* – selling practices, investment advice, suitability and professional aptitudes (de Manuel & Valiante, 2013). These elements are addressed with varying depth by the current EU regulatory and supervisory framework, as considered in the remainder of this section.

Product rules exist for UCITS funds and have been proposed for closed-end funds invested in less-liquid asset classes and open to retail clients, under the denomination ELTIF (European long-term investment funds – Box 3, above). The revision of MiFID (markets in financial instruments Directive), proposed by the European Commission, introduces a duty of *suitability at product design*, that would need to be developed in secondary legislation.[80] However, no product structuring rules exist for (defined contribution) pension solutions, nor any principles serving as guidelines for the application of a suitability duty at the structuring stage – section 3.4 proposes a blueprint to address these failures. In addition, MiFID provisions are not universally applied to all PRIPs (packaged retail investment products).[81]

As regards pre-contractual disclosure, the European Commission proposed in 2013 the introduction a standardised key information document (KID), initially

---

The emotional consequences of investing in the absence of guarantees can indeed induce great worry and tension on individuals, increasing the probability of sub-optimal decisions. The importance of emotional resilience is more pronounced when investing in the long-term (Professor Fenton-O'Creevy, presenting at a Task Force meeting).

[80] *Suitability at product design* refers to the set of principles, policies, processes and controls that should guide the design of financial products, in view of the client group to which each product is targeted (de Manuel and Valiante, 2013, IOSCO, 2012 and 2013). Article 9.6.d of the proposal to recast Directive 2004/39/EC [COM (2011) 656 final] places responsibility on senior management to define, approve and oversee the policy governing the services and products offered by the firm, in accordance with the characteristics and needs of the clients to whom the products will be offered or provided.

[81] PRIPs may be defined as retail investment solutions that entail: i) investment risk for the buyer, meaning the payout of the product depends on the market value of given assets, and ii) packaging, meaning that the assets are not held directly by the investor but rather are the underlying or reference assets to the end product. See European Commission (2009b), de Manuel (2012) and COM (2012) 352 final.

only for packaged retail investment products.[82] The KID will provide summary information in plain language under headings such as *What is this investment? What are the risks? What might I get back? What are the costs?* The objectives are to facilitate conscious purchases by retail investors and enable comparison within product categories (for instance, UCTIS A vs. UCITS B) and across product categories (ELTIF X vs. 'DC pension solution' Y) (de Manuel, 2012).

As regards long-term investing, pre-contractual disclosure documents should contain information, in subsequent layers, about: i) investment horizons and recommended holding periods, ii) the duration, redemption policy or liquidity profile of solution units, iii) in relation to the investment policy applied, whether it includes elements such as instruments with long maturities, strategic equity stakes or less-liquid assets; iv) whether a relative a short-term benchmark or a long-term absolute return objective is pursued; and v) whether the solution has an specific retirement objective or other specific long-term investing purpose. Pre-contractual disclosure should support communication for solutions with a distinct long-term investing purpose, such as ELTIFs – explaining potential benefits and drawbacks. The KID should contain referrals to other documents and sources, where needed to avoid information overload.

Pre-contractual disclosure needs to be complemented by ongoing disclosure, in particular for long-term saving/investing and retirement solutions. The longer the investment horizon, the higher the importance of periodic disclosure – both to keep investors informed and ensure that the incentives for providers remain aligned with the best interests of clients across the full length of the investment horizon. For defined contribution (and hybrid) retirement solutions, periodic statements should revolve around: i) retirement goals, phrased for instance as the monthly income targeted at retirement and ii) any action that members may undertake to increase the likelihood of achieving those goals. Conversely, it should avoid focusing on short-term volatility in accumulated values – during most of the accumulation phase, before it enters the final stage where pronounced drops in market prices would have a detrimental effect on the actual retirement income achieved (in the case of conversion into annuities). Otherwise, investors have been shown to react irrationally to short-term volatility and perceived losses in DC schemes, including by stopping any retirement savings altogether (Horack et al., 2010b). Similarly, where ongoing disclosure emphasises market values, managers have an incentive to centre their efforts on mitigating volatility rather than delivering returns over the investment horizon in line with the purpose of the retirement vehicle. Both retirement goals and market values are however important – the challenge

---

[82] COM (2012) 352 final.

therefore lies in finding a format of disclosure that achieves a good balance. Moreover, disclosure on an ongoing basis should also cover all costs.

Despite its importance, notably for long-term savings and retirement solutions, the EU framework for retail investor protection contains few provisions and no standards for ongoing disclosure. The absence of ongoing disclosure disables the ongoing assessment of suitability (where applicable) and reduces the control of ongoing costs incurred by providers (Box 7). In the field of retirement solutions, different standards are applied at national level, some of which pay insufficient regard to retirement goals and effective communication (Antolín & Harrison, 2012). In an effort to raise the quality of communications via soft coordination, EIOPA (2013f) put forward general guidance on good practices for information disclosure in defined contribution schemes, aimed at national supervisors and solution providers. The guidance emphasises the need to assist beneficiaries and to take full account of cognitive and behavioural limitations, and proposes to structure information in subsequent layers (Table 6).

Table 6. Checklist for drafting information requirements

Preparation	1	Have a behavioural purpose
	2	Provide a first layer of information that answers key questions
	3	Ensure information is retrievable
	4	Ensure the information provided is comprehensible
Drafting	5	Optimise attention
	6	Reduce complexity
	7	Provide figures that enable personal assessment and understanding
	8	Show potential implications of risks and ways to deal with them
	9	Support readers as much as possible towards financial decisions
Testing	10	Ensure thorough testing among members

Source: EIOPA (2013f).

Turning to sales practices, MiFID distinguishes *advised sales* – where the seller delivers a personal recommendation and needs to assess the suitability of the product for each buyer – and *non-advised sales* – where only an assessment of whether the buyer has the experience and knowledge to understand the risks involved in the transaction (appropriateness) is made. Some products are classified by MiFID as non-complex and hence can be purchased on an *execution-only* basis, exempted from any test in the sales process.[83] This framework presents both obstacles and opportunities to foster the access of retail investors to long-term investing and retirement solutions:

○ The MiFID framework fully ignores costs and fails to acknowledge that the quality of any personal recommendation or suitability assessment depends on the range of solutions and originators considered by the seller, its level of expertise and the alignment of incentives among seller and buyer.[84] In long-term and retirement savings, however, costs merit full consideration in view of their cumulative impact on net performance, and they should hence become an integral part of the suitability test (FSA, 2009).[85] Moreover, where the seller surveys solutions from only a narrow number of providers, any advice delivered is unlikely to incorporate any meaningful comparison of relevant features, including costs. In such instances, investors should at least be warned of the limitations of the 'advice' service received (de Manuel & Valiante, 2013).

○ The execution-only exemption opens a window of opportunity to widen the accessibility of long-term investing and retirement solutions for less well-off individuals. In effect, the cost of distribution and quality advice are sizeable and can significantly erode net returns. Yet, the availability of a solution for purchase by retail investors on an execution-only basis should be granted

---

[83] Articles 35 and 36, Directive 2006/73/EC, and Article 19.6, Directive 2004/39/EC. See de Manuel & Valiante (2013) for further reference.

[84] Regulation also needs to limit conflicts of interest in distribution and, in particular, for investment advice. MiFID I prohibits inducements but grants an exemption based on three conditions: i) it is designed to improve the quality of the service, ii) it does not impair the ability to act in the best interest of investors and iii) is appropriately disclosed (Article 26, Directive 2006/73/EC). Compliance with these conditions is so difficult to monitor and supervise that they almost strip the general prohibition from its meaning (de Manuel & Valiante, 2013). MiFID II is expected to introduce a reserved label for 'independent investment advice' that does not accept inducements. Challenges remain, including: i) facilitating the access to high quality advice among less wealthy individuals, by reducing the cost of this service, and ii) addressing the professional aptitudes of advisers.

[85] The UK Financial Services Authority (FSA) developed in 2009 a template for advisors to assess the suitability of pension-switching advice, which gives due consideration to costs:

Key unsuitable outcome 1: The customer has been switched to a pension that is more expensive than their existing one or a stakeholder pension (because of exit penalties and/or initial costs and ongoing costs of the receiving scheme versus the old scheme or a stakeholder pension) without good reason. [...] You should consider the total costs of the receiving scheme (including initial and ongoing fees) to be able to judge how these compare with the receiving scheme. – FSA (2009).

only on the basis of targeted product structuring rules. These rules should ensure that such solutions are adequate for retail investors to access without an individual assessment of suitability. Product rules would need to ensure the simplicity and quality of solutions, together with high standardisation,[86] to facilitate understanding and comparability. Box 5 (above) builds on these elements with reference to balanced funds and section 3.4 with respect to defined contribution personal pensions.

The harmonisation of investor protection rules is rather loose in Europe, with the exception of pre-contractual disclosure requirements.[87] Such fragmentation is thought to raise distribution costs for some investors and represents a barrier for investment solutions to gather efficient scale. European investors should be the prime beneficiaries of member states converging to a single but ambitious approach to the distribution of investment solutions, including long-term investment (de Manuel & Valiante, 2013).

2.4 A single market for direct investments

Pooled investments allow retail investors to benefit from diversification, expert asset allocation and risk management. The costs of intermediation should be compensated by these benefits, in a competitive and efficient market setting. Investors may however also access underlying securities directly, not pooling their savings together. Direct access allows end investors to save on the costs derived from solution structuring and some layers of intermediation, which may lead to higher net returns. However, direct access entails additional risks in comparison to pooled solutions, as far as non-professional investors tend to: i) have less knowledge and expertise than professionals, ii) suffer from more acute behavioural biases and iii) be unable to diversify, given the limited size of their portfolios, taken in isolation. In addition, direct access may result in opportunity costs, as a result of sub-optimal asset allocation, diversification or investment practices.

---

[86] Higher standardisation reduces the need for investment advice and may allow for the sale of such solutions on an execution-only basis and upon publicly-provisioned information. Conversely, product proliferation and differentiation make the choice more difficult by raising the need for professional advice. Both sorts of solutions (standardised and customised), however, add value to investor choice and may co-exist in the marketplace. The distinction between execution-only and advised sales may be utilised to distinguish both sorts of solutions, as a tool to better structure the market setting.

[87] EU rules on investor protection are also scattered across multiple legislative instruments, which does not help consistency either (notably, selling practices are regulated separately in MiFID and the IMD – the insurance mediation Directive).

In spite of the caveats above, direct access to certain securities, notably simple bonds and equities, may deal positive results for retail investors with sufficient expertise. Direct access may deal more attractive returns than pooled solutions, although strict comparison is not possible, as returns should be weighted on a risk-adjusted basis.[88] Capital markets and the 'real' economy may also benefit from facilitating direct access by small retail investors to bonds and equities. Such investors are thought to provide in particular a source of stable and long-term finance, by for instance holding bonds to maturity. Expert investors may also sidestep agency conflicts in the asset management value chain by directly investing their capital.

In Europe access to equities is relatively easy for small retail clients, in spite of which concerns remain regarding retail investor protection and best execution policies, among others (Valiante & Lannoo, 2011). By way of contrast, bond markets are predominantly institutional and access for retail investors is fairly limited in Europe. Notable exceptions are found in a few member states, where certain corporate and sovereign bonds are accessible to retail clients – typically limited to bonds issued by entities domiciled in that member state. The lack of a single market restricts the free flow of capital and unduly restricts choice for retail investors, as well as the potential financing available to companies. From a practical point of view, widening retail access to bond markets would require a rethink of market structure, including the levels of transparency prevalent in the marketplace. However important, these questions exceed the remit of this report.[89]

---

[88] While it has been argued that the (high) fees charged by solution providers sometimes exceed the benefits of pooling and expertise (Eurofinuse, 2013), this argument elicits rather the importance of a competitive setting and market structure. The objective of policy-makers should be to enable access to cost-efficient pooled solutions, given the objective benefits of, professionally managed, pooled investments over undiversified direct access by non-expert investors.

[89] For a discussion on the level of transparency in bond markets and other issues regarding market structure refer to Valiante & Lannoo (2011). The authors also review the risks in bond investments (Box 5).

3. LONG-TERM INVESTING AND PERSONAL PENSIONS

Personal pension plans are defined by the OECD (2005) as private plans where "access *does not have to* be linked to an employment relationship".[90] These plans are established and administered directly by a qualifying private undertaking, without intervention from the employer (sponsor), as opposed to occupational plans.[91] In effect, personal pension plans or solutions are typically selected and purchased by individuals separately from their employment relationship. Employers "may nonetheless make contributions to personal pension plans" (OECD, 2005).

The dividing line between personal and occupational pensions is often blurred, as highlighted in the request from the European Commission (2012i) to EIOPA to deliver technical advice on developing a single market for personal pension schemes in the EU.[92] The request follows initiative thirteen in the White Paper on pensions (European Commission, 2012c) to raise the quality of third-pillar retirement products, possibly by introducing an EU certification scheme.

---

[90] Private plans are defined by the OECD (2005) as follows: "A pension plan administered by an institution other than general government. Private pension plans may be administered directly by a private sector employer acting as the plan sponsor, a private pension fund or a private sector provider. Private pension plans may complement or substitute for public pension plans. In some countries, these may include plans for public sector workers."

[91] Occupational plans are defined by the OECD (2005) as follows: "Access to such plans is linked to an employment or professional relationship between the plan member and the entity that establishes the plan (the plan sponsor). Occupational plans may be established by employers or groups thereof (e.g. industry associations) and labour or professional associations, jointly or separately. The plan may be administered directly by the plan sponsor or by an independent entity."

[92] "I think it is very important that personal pension schemes are considered in close connection with occupational pension schemes because the borderline between personal and occupational pensions is often blurred. [...] I invite EIOPA to engage in a second phase with a view to providing technical advice on the prudential regulation and consumer protection measures required to develop an EU-wide framework for the activities and supervision of personal pension funds. EIOPA's advice should consider at least two approaches: i) develop common rules to enable cross-border activity of personal pension schemes (similar to the IORP Directive); and ii) develop a 28th regime, whereby EU rules do not replace national rules but are an optional alternative to them." European Commission (2012i).

In this chapter, 'personal pensions' refers to defined contribution solutions and potentially other (hybrid) arrangements offered by financial intermediaries. It therefore excludes traditional defined benefit occupational schemes. Yet, it is meant to encompass plans to which employers may make contributions, while being easily portable for the plan holder when changing employer.

This chapter argues that raising the quality of solution design within personal pensions entails fostering long-term investing practices and embedding a clear vision about retirement goals. The chapter is structured as follows: section 3.1 presents some key observations on the situation of private pensions in Europe today, referring to their increasingly important but diverse role, insufficient coverage and low contributions, and sometimes high costs and low returns. Section 3.2 considers the market structure and proposes an enabling industrial policy. Section 3.3 exposes potential shortcomings in solution design and key trade-offs. And section 3.4 concludes by proposing a blueprint for a pan-European framework for personal pensions.

3.1 Private pensions in Europe today

An increasingly important but diverse role...

The role and coverage of personal pension plans vary widely across the EU, as a result of the diversity of pension policies and multi-pillar mixes developed in member states over time. Nevertheless, defined contribution (DC) and personal schemes play an increasingly important role in pension systems – as employers phase out the provision of defined benefits (DB), unwilling or unable to bear market and longevity risks, and ageing reduces the funding available for traditional public pensions, based on taxation or social contributions and redistribution (Holzmann, 2012).[93] Moreover, some member

---

[93] The high replacement rates traditionally afforded by public provision are unlikely to be delivered in the future, given demographic changes, including longer life expectancy and lower fertility rates, leading to an ageing population. To reduce (or at least contain the growth of) unaccounted pension liabilities and ensure the sustainability of social security systems, EU member states have been progressively reforming pension systems over the last decade, under the political steering and technical guidance of the European Commission, the European Council and international organisations such as the OECD.

The 2008 financial crisis and the subsequent contagion to sovereign debt markets in the euro area have accelerated the need both for reform (given the deterioration of public finances) and closer macroeconomic coordination among member states, particularly within the euro currency union. The reform of PAYG (pay as you go)systems is therefore still ongoing and is likely to deepen, notably with the inclusion of automatic adjustment mechanisms for paid benefits in line with life expectancy and funding (so-called 'sustainability factors') – and this

states have introduced defined contribution schemes within the system of public provision (so-called 'pillar one-bis schemes', which sometimes incorporate minimum return guarantees).

With the exception of DB meta-schemes, DC and hybrid plans tend to be better adapted to job mobility than traditional (final salary) DB schemes, which the employee typically cannot carry with him or her when changing employer. Portability is not just a challenging and costly administrative issue but has further consequences in terms of sub-optimal asset allocation (scattered through multiple and uncoordinated pension pots) and opportunity costs.

Given the absence of guarantees, DC and hybrid solutions have the potential of delivering better risk-adjusted returns and more efficient asset allocation than traditional DB and life-insurance solutions (section 1.4). However, the design and the provision of personal DC pensions are affected by a number of frictions, which tend to result in poor results for beneficiaries, as considered in this chapter. While the growing importance of DC and hybrid solutions is a common theme in Europe, there remains great diversity. Despite this diversity however, a number of common challenges are identified and discussed in the next sections. These challenges are i) insufficient coverage and contributions, ii) high costs and iii) low returns. After describing these challenges, the rest of the chapter is devoted to their underlying causes from the points of view of solution design and market structure. The chapter ends by proposing a blueprint for a pan-European framework for personal pensions.

Insufficient coverage and low contributions...

While the data are difficult to access, the move from DB to DC in the occupational space seems to be accompanied by a decrease in contributions, in a manner that may fail to ensure adequate replacement rates for households relying on occupational schemes as their primary source of income in retirement. In the United Kingdom for instance, the size of average contributions in occupational DC schemes is roughly half the size in DB schemes.[94]

Similarly in non-occupational space, low contributions are coupled with low participation. Table 7 presents the rates of participation and median

---

despite the non-inclusion so far of unaccounted pension liabilities in the Stability and Growth Pact. On the transparency of public pension liabilities, see Cocquemas (2013).

[94] For private sector occupational DB schemes, the average contribution rate was 4.9% for members (employees) and 14.2% for employers in 2011, while the rates for DC schemes were 2.8% and 6.6%, respectively. In the UK the move from DB to DC has also been accompanied by a decrease in coverage – there were 8.2 million active members in 2011, compared to 11.1 million in 1983 (Office for National Statistics, 2012).

accumulated values in voluntary private pension plans and life insurance in Europe. Participation and median accumulated values will be typically lower in countries with higher coverage and benefits from occupational schemes and public pensions. Yet, at aggregate level, looking at income and net wealth, the data reveal the existence of three investor categories:

- Households in the *lowest deciles* exhibit the lowest participation and values – below 20% and €5,000 respectively. Most of these households cannot afford to save and are better helped by public anti-poverty safety nets than by complementary pensions.
- Households in the *highest deciles* exhibit the highest participation and values – below 60% and €30,000 respectively. These households are better served by customised investment solutions, other than mass-market solutions.
- Households in the *middle deciles* exhibit middle participation and values – between 20% and 40% and €5,000 to €15,000. These households can afford to save and would benefit the most from building a personal pension – as they typically cannot access complementary public benefits or afford investment solutions, other than mass-market ones.

Crucially, Table 7 shows that coverage and contributions are low even for households in the *middle deciles,* despite the fact that these households are in a better financial position to save. Approximately 80% to 60% of these households do not hold a complementary pension solution and, among those that do, the median accumulated value is €20,600 at retirement (ECB, 2013).[95]

Table 7. Participation in voluntary private pensions and life insurance

	Percentile of EA income					Percentile of EA net wealth					Education			Home ownership		
	>20	20-39	40-59	60-79	80-100	>20	20-39	40-59	60-79	80-100	Primary	Secondary	Tertiary	Owner	Mortgage	Renter
Participation (in percent)	13.2	20.4	31.1	41.9	58.3	15.9	32.7	31.5	35.8	49.1	19.0	36.4	46.8	28.9	47.8	30.1
Median value (€ thousands)	4.4	5.1	8.6	11.8	23.0	1.6	6.4	11.8	14.2	29.1	9.2	10.1	17.5	16.1	15.0	6.6

Notes: Data for Belgium, Germany, Greece, Spain, France, Italy, Cyprus, Luxembourg, Malta, the Netherlands, Austria, Portugal, Slovenia, Slovakia and Finland. EA refers to euro area.
Source: Eurosystem Household Finance and Consumption Survey (ECB, 2013).

---

[95] Median accumulated value for households where the main person is aged 63 to 67 years old [Variables PF0920 and RA0300 in the Eurosystem Household Finance and Consumption Survey (ECB, 2013)].

The optimal level of contributions in DC schemes depends on net returns[96] and the replacement rate (or recurring income during retirement) sought by the individual. Where it comes to complementary pensions, the optimal level of contributions depends therefore on the replacement rate expected from the principal sources of retirement income – occupational schemes and public pensions. Additional disclosure and research are needed to measure the actual underfunding of expected replacement rates and to inform individuals. Yet, the limited evidence available provides a strong indication that current participation and contributions are unlikely to meet the expectations of and future needs of beneficiaries. Figure 18 illustrates that over 50% of the population in the UK, France and Germany save 5% or less of their yearly income for retirement, while still expecting to retire at around age 65.

Figure 18. Retirement expectations vs. contribution levels

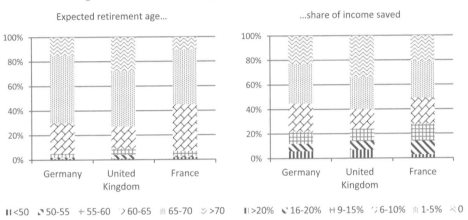

Source: Boston Consulting Group.

Tax incentives are frequently used by governments to encourage contributions to private pension plans and discourage redemptions before retirement. Such incentives have however a cost for public finances and benefit investor cohorts unequally. Most forms of tax incentives tend to benefit the wealthier cohorts of individuals. Conversely, low income cohorts benefit less, even though they are the most in need. Compulsory savings are thought to be a more efficient tool to increase saving rates. They also free up public resources that can be better used to top-up savings by low incomes and reduce financial exclusion in the market for long-term and retirement savings (Chetty et al., 2012).

---

[96] The higher the net returns (market returns minus fees and costs), the more the accumulated savings will grow over time without additional contributions.

High costs and low returns...

> When advising people to save more, public authorities should bear in mind that pension saving products are in many cases destroying real value of citizens' savings. This is why providers and public authorities should seek to protect the long-term purchasing power of savings, before advising citizens to increase those.
>
> Eurofinuse (2013).

Private pensions are generally, despite their different forms, at the forefront of popular criticism of the financial industry, regarding its failure to deliver value to clients. And the limited evidence available points indeed at dismal and even negative returns (net of costs) for investors, on average in the last decade. Low market returns are mostly to blame but administration and investment costs are also believed to be prime drivers.[97]

Aggregate statistics on returns and costs are rare. By way of illustration, Figure 19 presents the average investment return of collective pension funds in selected OECD economies, net of inflation and observed costs. In Europe, net returns were on average slightly positive from 2001 and 2010, below 2% for the countries listed. Returns were positive in all countries, except in Spain, the UK and the US. Following the financial crisis and the economic recession, returns turned negative, except in Denmark and Germany (OECD, 2012). The data, however, refer to a relatively short time-frame for pension accumulation, which should typically last for over 30 years.

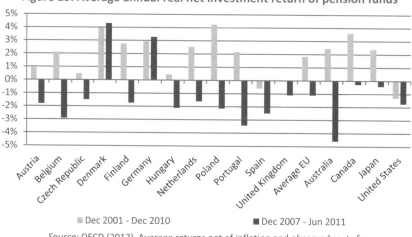

Figure 19. Average annual real net investment return of pension funds

■ Dec 2001 - Dec 2010   ■ Dec 2007 - Jun 2011

Source: OECD (2012). Average returns net of inflation and observed costs for collective pension funds, excluding individual private pension products.

---

[97] The term 'cost' refers in this section all fees, charges and costs leading to a reduction in net returns, in comparison to underlying market returns.

International comparisons of performance are difficult given the diversity of pension solutions, fee structures and disclosure standards (OECD, 2011d; Hernandez & Stewart, 2008; Tapia & Yermo, 2008). However, evidence at national level is indicative of average fee levels and their dispersion. By way of illustration, annual management fees, applied yearly to the value accumulated assets, near 0.13% in the Netherlands on average while they exceed 0.70% in the United Kingdom (AFM, 2011; DWP, 2012).

Depending chiefly on the volume of assets of the pension solution, annual fees can vary widely. In the Netherlands, the average management fee for small funds nears 1.20% – 12 times the average fee for the largest funds (AFM, 2011). Similarly, in the UK, average fees for the smallest funds exceed 1%, while they fall below 0.50% for the biggest funds (DWP, 2012).

In addition to annual management fees disclosed up-front, investment costs also add up to total ongoing expenses for pension solutions. Disclosure of the latter is however more cumbersome, as it is necessarily ex-post and sometimes difficult to observe and compile – in particular for underlying funds, complex derivatives and structured instruments (Box 7). Actual investment costs may therefore be multiples of the figures reported.[98]

A moderate difference in costs can however lead to a substantial difference in benefits. This is particularly true for ongoing costs, applied on a yearly basis on the accumulated value of the investment, both principal and returns. Figure 20 compares the impact of different yearly cost rates on total net returns and total costs at the end of a thirty-year investment horizon. Under high cost rates, total costs may exceed net returns by a multiple. Contributions, cost rates and return rates are assumed to be yearly and constant (Table A.2 in the annex).

Most retail investors have problems understanding the effects of compounding and the final impact of what they may perceive as small differences in ongoing charges (Charter et al., 2010; Lusardi et al., 2006). Cost transparency, however, does not only affect investor choice but also incentives for intermediaries, and competition dynamics (Box 7).

---

[98] The Dutch supervisor estimates that the average investment cost reported (0.19%) is actually two to three times larger (0.38% - 0.57%). The problem is more acute among smaller pension funds, as they have less bargaining power to enforce transparency from asset managers and originators and tend to lack the expertise and infrastructure for effective cost accounting with full look-through to the costs embedded in underlying investment funds, derivative instruments and structured products (AFM, 2011).

Figure 20. Impact of different cost rates on net returns at year thirty

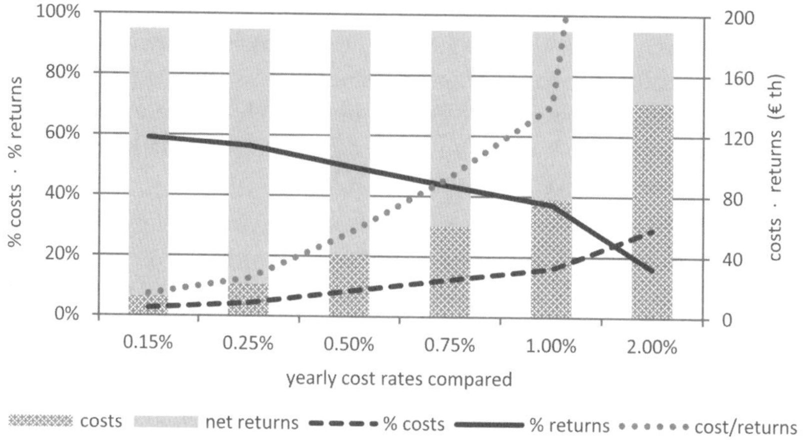

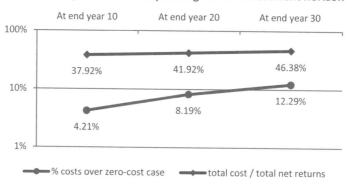

Source: Author. Balance of total costs and net returns after having invested €10,000 per year over 30 years, assuming a yearly rate of return of 3% on accumated assets. See Table A.2 in the annex for a full reference on this simplified investment case.

The compounding of ongoing costs also means that their impact increases over time. The longer the investment horizon, the higher the impact of yearly costs on total costs, both in relative and absolute terms. By way of illustration, building on the simple scenario above, Figure 21 presents the relative effect of a 0.75% yearly cost rate after 10, 20 and 30 years. The share of total costs at the end of each investment horizon, in comparison with total returns in the zero-cost case (benchmark) increases by eight percentage points over 20 years, from 4% to 12% due to compounding.

Figure 21. Impact of costs depending on the investment horizon

Source: Author. See Table A.2 in the annex for a full reference.

Against the background of low returns in the marketplace, the crucial question is whether efficiency and innovation can help deliver better value to investors.

The following two sections will consider: i) how an enabling industrial policy, which addresses market structure, may help drive both cost savings and innovation, and ii) how solution design and asset allocation may be better aligned with retirement goals and long-term horizons, to deliver potentially higher returns and better serve the needs of investors. The last section presents a blueprint for pan-European personal pensions.

Box 6. Interim conclusions from the UK Office of Fair Trading

In 2013, the UK Office of Fair Trading (OFT) launched a study on the market for defined contribution workplace pensions, in view of the expected increase in participation after the introduction of auto-enrolment in 2012. The purpose of the study is to examine whether the market is serving consumers well, and whether supply and competition dynamics are working in the best interest of investors, by delivering low-cost, high-quality schemes. On 11 July 2013, the OFT issued the following conclusions in a progress update:

- The current level of governance over the performance of some schemes may not be sufficient to ensure that scheme members are getting the best possible investment outcomes.

- A number of schemes have been set up with two-tier charging structures, where those members who have stopped making contributions pay a higher annual management charge percentage.

- There are a number of schemes open for auto-enrolment that appear to have built-in adviser commissions and which may not represent the best value for money for those that could be enrolled into them.

- There may be a number of schemes that do not have a realistic prospect of reaching sufficient scale to generate value for their members.

- The way that different providers currently present their charges may mean that they are not easily comparable.

- There may be some schemes – primarily but not exclusively those sold prior to 2001 – that have charges that may not represent the best value for money, or that may not reflect current standards of scheme design.

Box 7. Cost transparency, incentives and competition

Cost transparency is seen as an essential element of investor protection, helping investors make informed decisions and promoting competition in the marketplace (see section 2.3). However, cost transparency not only affects investor choice but also contributes to shape incentives for providers and intermediaries.

A broad distinction can be made between headline *administrative* charges, known ex-ante and incorporating the commercial margin of the intermediary originating the product, and *investment* costs, which depend on the actual implementation of the investment mandate by the originator and can only be observed ex-post. In addition, *distribution and advisory* charges also apply.

Investment costs are frequently difficult to observe and compile. Transparency is more cumbersome for providers to enforce when investing in pooled vehicles[a] – particularly if restricted to institutional investors, where retail disclosure standards do not apply – and complex derivative transactions and structured instruments – whose pricing process is, by the very nature of these instruments, opaque. These are frequently known as 'second-floor fees'.

Any investment decision should be made on the basis of costs, and not only by risk-adjusted returns. Yet, the ability of solution-providers to enforce full cost transparency on intermediaries depends on their bargaining power and relative size (AFM, 2011). And even where costs are known, compilation and processing require resources that many providers lack, in particular smaller ones (AFM, 2011).

In some market segments, most *investment* costs are not explicitly reported but directly deducted from net returns and net asset values (AFM, 2011). Partial disclosure casts doubts as to whether these costs are effectively taken into account and monitored by providers. Deficient cost accounting and disclosure ultimately distort incentives for providers (Figure 22). And may also foster related party transactions, among entities belonging to a same group, in less competitive markets.

Figure 22. Full versus partial cost transparency and related incentives

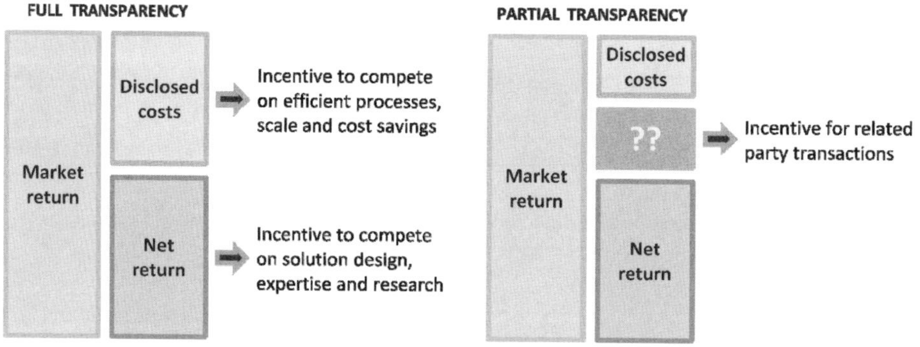

Source: Author.

Next to cost accounting and disclosure, the unbundling of costs categories can also act as an important driver for efficiencies. It has been estimated that approximately only 45% to 50% of management fees are retained by the originators of retail investment funds in Europe, with the remainder being paid back to distributors and advisors (EFAMA and Strategic Insight, 2011). Making the costs of distribution services transparent to investors could help achieve further cost reductions over time.[b]

Regulation and supervision play important roles in fostering effective cost accounting and transparency throughout the investment management value chain:

○ For end investors, a simple and uniform structure/presentation of fees for all solutions in the marketplace has been shown to improve transparency and stimulate competition (IFF Research et al., 2009). At the point of sale, pre-contractual disclosure should capture all costs known ex-ante and an estimation of those costs that can only be known ex-post.[c] Periodic disclosure of actual costs should follow suit on an ongoing basis (Figure 23).

○ For providers, additional action is needed to facilitate effective cost accounting and the factoring of costs into investment decisions. The right of originators to demand full cost transparency from intermediaries should be reinforced, including by creating effective enforcement mechanisms. And cost accounting should be explicitly recognised as a duty for providers, auditors and supervisors to control, as considered in this report.

Yet, price transparency is no silver bullet as its positive impact on competition is limited by the inability of many investors (or pension plan holders) to understand fees in isolation, let alone apprehend their cumulative impact over time (Charter et al., 2010). Additional market structure measures are arguably needed to drive cost efficiencies forward (section 3.2).

Figure 23. Reported versus non-reported costs and main policy tools

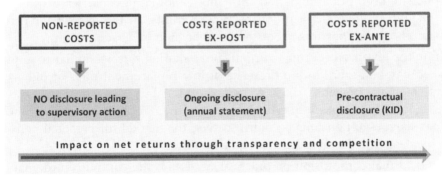

Source: Author.

----

[a] Without prejudice to the high level of disclosure provided by some forms of pooled vehicles, including notably pre-contractual disclosure for UCITS funds under the regulated KIID standard.

[b] Making the costs of distribution transparent is important, whether these costs are embedded in overall fees for the investment solution or the charges for distribution and/or investment advice are unbundled (as in the United Kingdom following the Retail Distribution Review and planned in other member states). Originators should have the responsibility for disclosing the costs related to the product or solution itself while distributors should have the responsibility of disclosing the costs related to distribution, aggregating all costs and communicating them to investors. Investors should be able to access a total cost figure, summing up both product and distribution costs, comparable across products/solutions and sale channels/services.

[c] This is the principle followed in the standardised disclosure of ongoing charges for UCITS funds, which is based on actual costs from the preceding year (art.78.3.d Directive 2009/65/EC, Commission Regulation 583/2010 and ESMA Guidelines CESR/10-673).

3.2   Addressing market structure: An enabling industry policy

> If the market structure is such as to give the right incentive, then appropriate behaviour should follow, and regulatory oversight of such behaviour can be reduced: if market structure and incentives are not right, then regulation which imposes behaviour which conflicts with the commercial interests of participants is likely to enjoy limited success.
>
> Kay (2012).

Demand and diversity of cohorts...

The characteristics of demand for private pensions depend on the institutional setting for the provision of retirement income in each jurisdiction. Where demand is compulsory or semi-compulsory, a quasi-market is found, meaning demand is captive, as it cannot choose to abstain from consumption (Impavido et al., 2010). A typical example is the use of private pensions as part of pillar one provision in some of the member states of the European Union.[99]

Captive consumers are at a higher risk of exploitation by the supply side of the market. A captive demand facilitates the explicit or tacit coordination of suppliers to keep prices high and stifle innovation, unless barriers to entry are low enough to enable disruption by new entrants. In the market for private pensions however, barriers to entry tend to be high (next subsection).

Even in the absence of formal compulsion, a market setting similar to a quasi-market may be found. In the presence of low replacement rates in pillar one, complementary pensions cease to be an option but a practical necessity to achieve income adequacy in retirement. Over the next decades, as the funding for pay-as-you-go pensions becomes scarcer, the market for personal pensions will increasingly resemble a perfect quasi-market.[100]

Beyond formal compulsion or practical necessity, the captivity of demand is also explained by its low elasticity (response function) to both solution quality and price. The complexity and asymmetries of information present in the market place are exacerbated by the limited ability of demand to understand solution features and their implications. As a result of behavioural and

---

[99] Pillar one-bis schemes exist in the following EU member states: Bulgaria, Czech Republic, Denmark, Latvia, Hungary, Lithuania, Poland, Romania, Slovak Republic and Sweden (Eichhorst et al., 2011; Oxera, 2007). Participation and contribution to pillar one-bis schemes is compulsory. Schemes are administered by privately managed undertakings, frequently in a competitive environment, and supplement or substitute traditional pillar one pensions (pay-as-you-go) (EIOPA, 2013h).

[100] In particular in those markets where occupational pensions do not exist, have insufficient coverage or afford inadequate replacement incomes.

cognitive and limitations, individuals are unlikely to shop around or change providers (Charter et al., 2010).

It does not, however, help to simplify demand as if it were a homogenous group. Quite the opposite, demand is diverse – even though probably not as diverse as the level of product proliferation in some market segments would indicate (Celerier & Vallee, 2012). Demand can usefully be grouped in three cohorts, in accordance to their wealth, salience and behaviour; each of which requires differentiated policy action (Table 8).

Table 8. Stylised characterisation of investor cohorts

#	Financial means	Behaviour	Salience	Applicable policy solutions
1	CAN'T afford to save	WON'T save since they have peremptory needs	SHOULDN'T be confronted with investment markets	◦Rely on public provision and anti-poverty mechanisms
2	CAN afford to save	PROBABLY WILL save	COULD become informed consumers	◦Need an efficient market structure ◦May need incentives ◦Benefit from financial education
3	CAN afford to invest	WILL invest to build / maximise wealth	ARE informed investors	◦Need choice and customisation ◦Do not need incentives

Source: Author based on Task Force discussions and Clark et al. (2012).

Policy-makers and industry should be mindful of the features and size of each cohort. Individuals with low income or wealth, at risk of falling into poverty and unable to save, will rely primarily on anti-poverty safety nets financed by taxation or social contributions. While at the opposite end of the scale, high net worth individuals can readily access high-quality advice and custom solutions. The largest cohort of individuals, however, can afford to save only marginally and needs an efficient market structure, capable of delivering high-quality and cost-efficient solutions.

Supply and competition dynamics...

Supply and competition dynamics for private pensions are shaped by barriers to entry and scale economies, as well as switching costs. For personal pensions, the combined effect of these market failures pushes supply and competition dynamics towards product proliferation (over pooling of solutions and quality in solution design) and cost inefficiencies (derived from fragmentation and marketing expenditure).

By making disruption by new entrants unlikely, entry barriers lead to higher mark-ups and are a disincentive to further efficiencies and innovation. A major barrier to entry is the volume of assets under management required to reach efficient scale in the administration of private pensions. A high efficient scale makes disruption by new entrants unlikely unless supported by sufficient balance-sheet capacity or grandfathered by regulators. Entry for small players is easier in functions with lower scale economies, such as asset management,[101] but may not deliver competitive pricing unless administration is pooled.

Switching costs focus competition on attracting customers (through marketing expenditure) since once an investor enters a solution, s/he is unlikely to move out. Switching costs include: i) transaction costs – such as search, information and learning costs, derived from information asymmetries, cognitive limitations and the complexity of solutions and market settings, ii) exit costs – such as exit fees, penalties or conditional rebates on bundled products; iii) uncertainty costs – due to the experience and credence attributes of investment and insurance solutions;[102] and iv) behavioural biases – including procrastination.

The switching costs above are exogenous to long-term investing and can hence be addressed, even partially, by measures such as: standardising information, facilitating access to advice, prohibiting penalties and bundling or introducing minimum qualitative requirements for any solution sold.

At a structural level, however, long-term investing requires a level of illiquidity towards investors (regarding redemptions and transfers) that can be seen both as an opportunity and switching cost. Investors need to forego the opportunity for immediate redemptions in order to access the potential for higher risk-adjusted returns at retirement (opportunity cost). And easy switching is not possible without renouncing the premiums linked to long-term investing strategies and illiquid underlyings (switching cost).

As a result of those entry barriers and switching costs, supply and competition dynamics may focus on product proliferation (trial and error, segmentation) and marketing (branding, spurious differentiation) over solution quality, cost efficiencies (scale) and eased investor access (simplicity in solution design and

---

[101] In comparison with the administration and processing functions, which have high scale economies and may benefit from centralisation for a given market, the asset management function has relatively lower scale economies, except in relation to back-office functions and the access to specialised or illiquid asset classes, in view of the needs for qualified expertise and diversification.

[102] In an experience good, quality can only be observed after consumption. In a credence good, quality cannot be observed even after consumption (de Manuel & Valiante, 2013). Experience and credence attributes introduce an upward pressure in prices, since the inability to observe performance brings investors to infer higher quality from higher prices, and facilitate product proliferation based on branding and other spurious factors. They also explain the weight carried by 'trust' in determining investment decisions.

choice environment). They also may forego long-term investing practices and holdings of less-liquid assets in favour of high liquidity for clients (in terms of redemptions) – as the bespoke benefits from long-term investing can only be observed in the long run. It has been argued that these failures are generalised in the wider (retail) asset management industry and cannot be effectively addressed but though structural measures (Kay, 2012).

As the demand for complementary pensions becomes less of a choice and more of a necessity for individuals, a quasi-market will be found, bearing a practical obligation for welfare states to reduce distortions in supply and competition dynamics, by both addressing market structure and solution design (Impavido et al., 2010).

Box 8. Marketing and switching: The example of Poland

The experience from quasi-markets is that marketing expenses can significantly raise costs without delivering substantial benefits to investors (Tapia & Yermo, 2008; Impavido et al., 2010). Figure 24 presents the yearly transfers among the 14 open pension funds (OPFs) available in the Polish pillar one-bis system. OPFs are reported to have used aggressive marketing practices, involving the use of over 400,000 sales agents to encourage members to change plans (ILO, 2002). Under these practices, nearly 4% of participants switched providers at the peak, in 2010. Additional restrictions on sales practices were then introduced, in an effort to reduce marketing expenditure, and transfers collapsed in 2012.

Marketing and acquisition expenses (sales agents, new contracts and transfers) accounted for about 40% of total costs incurred by Open Pension Funds in the period 2007-11. In 2012, following the introduction of marketing restrictions, the weight of related expenses decreased to just 18% (Table 9). Despite the very considerable marketing expense and number of sale agents, a switching rate of 4% remains relatively low in comparison to other industries. For instance, estimations suggest that 10% of current-account holders in Europe changed providers in 2011 (GFK, 2011).

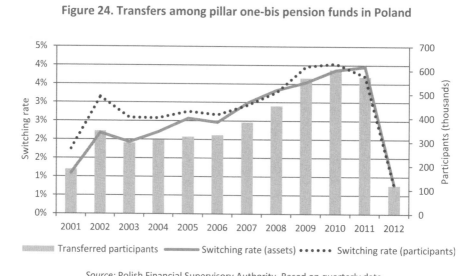

Figure 24. Transfers among pillar one-bis pension funds in Poland

Source: Polish Financial Supervisory Authority. Based on quarterly data.

Table 9. Acquisition and marketing costs of OPFs in Poland

	2012	2011	2010	2009	2008	2007	2000
Costs of acquisition	121.80	384.90	473.90	446.40	368.10	321.50	811.40
Marketing costs	9.90	8.50	23.10	37.00	42.20	39.60	68.00
Total management costs	728.20	1025.00	1242.30	1210.10	1050.00	968.20	1646.00
Share over total costs	18%	38%	40%	40%	39%	37%	53%

Source: Polish Central Statistical Office (GUS) and ILO (2002).

The role of processing architecture...

Individual countries have found different solutions to high costs and welfare-reducing marketing expenditure, including notably: i) putting grandfathered or not-for-profit institutions in direct competition with for-profit ones, and ii) opening competition for the market or sections of it, by way of procurement processes. An example of all these practices is the National Employee Savings Trust (NEST) introduced in the UK in 2012. NEST is a not-for-profit institution in competition with other market players, and has a public service obligation to serve any employers who wish to choose NEST as default option, to fulfil their obligations under the Pensions Act of 2008. In the Netherlands, not-for-profit entities, jointly managed by employers and employees (paritarian), also play a central role in pension provision.

Some other countries have employed more crude tools, such as imposing price caps and limits to switching across providers. However, these measures alone, fail to address the root causes of high costs, namely inefficiencies in supply and competition dynamics, and may have important unintended effects (Tapia & Yermo, 2008, Impavido et al., 2010): Price caps can be easily circumvented by the misreporting of investment costs and related party transactions (via second floor fees – see Box 7, above). Limits to aggressive marketing practices may be effective in reducing marketing expenditure but artificial limits to switching make consumers more captive and thereby introduce an upward pressure on fees. Limits to switching should be derived naturally – from the alignment of redemption policies with the liquidity profile of underlying assets and long-term investment practices, both for financial stability and investor protection reasons.

An appropriately designed processing architecture emerges as an efficient tool to reduce the focus of competition on marketing over solution quality and cost, while delivering a highly competitive market setting (Haupt & Kluth, 2013; Impavido et al., 2010; Guardiancich, 2010; Tapia & Yermo, 2008; Weaver, 2005). The example of the Swedish Premium Pension System is paramount in this respect. The use of a central clearing house means that administration costs are minimised, while facilitating comparability and switching across providers. Only the total invested sum is known by providers, rather than the identities of beneficiaries, reducing the incentive for aggressive marketing practices. As end investors are not communicated to providers, their only client is the Swedish Pension Agency, who has a greater bargaining power and is able to negotiate rebates in management fees, as asset under management grow, redistributing the benefits of scale economies.

Efficient scale and optimal bundling...

In addition to the benefits above, a single processing architecture would have greater potential if undertaken at pan-European level, as it could further drive scale through market integration. In most member states, current market size is insufficient to achieve efficient scale, in particular for long-term investing.

Pan-European scale should lead to: i) lower costs – as high fixed costs would be distributed among a greater number of participants; ii) more expertise in management and administration, business sophistication and innovation – as under efficient scale, the cost of these can be more easily afforded; and iii) direct access to certain asset classes, including less-liquid ones, which due to their complexity or the minimum size of the initial investment, require specific expertise and processing capabilities, and scale (assets under management) for diversification purposes. Figures 25 and 26 present the apparent effects of scale on administration expenses for defined contribution schemes in the UK and Germany.

Efficient scale, however, is reached at different points for each of the functions in the production chain for private pensions. The collection of contributions, administration and processing of subscriptions and redemptions benefits from the highest economies of scale, and may therefore be carried out by one central entity. Communications with end beneficiaries also benefit from economies of scale, in particular regarding the design of standard formats and their testing with consumers. By way of contrast, asset management benefits relatively less from economies of scale, in comparison to administration and processing, except for back-office functions. Yet, direct access to illiquid assets and private placements requires very large fund sizes, in terms of volume of assets under management, to achieve efficient diversification.

The bundling of services and functions with different efficient scale leads to inefficient outcomes – either higher total costs (where bundling takes place at a lower scale) or reduced choice (where bundling takes place at a higher scale). It is therefore essential that any industrial policy for private pensions strives to achieve optimal bundling. "If policy makers fail to establish institutions for the centralised provision and procurement of services with high economies of scale, barriers to entry will be artificially extended" (Impavido et al., 2010, p. 161).

Figure 25. Scale effects in DC schemes in the UK

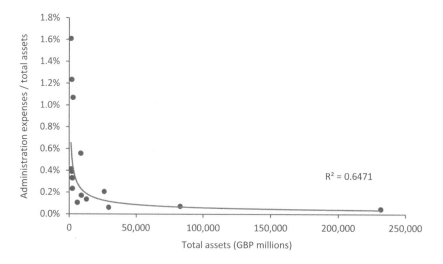

Source: BCG (based on own analysis and SynThesys). Data comprise all UK players with over GBP 1 bn assets, 100% pension share and over 95% DC share within pension.

Figure 26. Scale effects in DC schemes in Germany

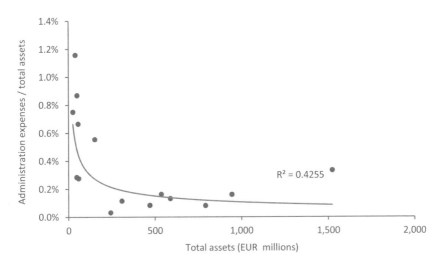

Source: BCG (based on own analysis and BaFin). Data comprise all German pension funds ('pensionsfonds') that report administration expenses with a DC share over 50%.

The single market potential...

The EU single market holds the potential to maximise scale economies while increasing the level of competition in the marketplace, delivering high-quality and low-cost pension solutions to beneficiaries. In addition, from a long-term investing perspective, high scale is needed to access less-liquid asset classes. A pan-European processing architecture would be central for both purposes. The experience with UCITS indicates that without a single processing architecture, the potential derived from market integration – in terms of cost efficiencies and choice for retail investors – cannot be exploited in full.

In practical terms, achieving a pan-European processing architecture would require some form of tax harmonisation, which could only affect the structure of taxation, while keeping tax rates as a matter for member states. The benefits would be numerous, both in terms of increased convergence at macroeconomic level, increased pension adequacy and investor protection, and eased cross-border mobility of workers, while promoting long-term investing though appropriate principles regarding solution design.

3.3 Addressing solution design: Long-term investing and retirement savings

Issues identified...

The market for private pensions may be characterised, in some of its segments, by the poor design of the solutions offered. A detailed assessment of solution design is not possible, given the lack of readily accessible and comparable information and the widely different institutional and market settings in which private pensions are delivered in Europe. Yet, discussions during the meetings of the Task Force and available literature point towards shortcomings in a number of areas, closely related to long-term investing:

○ *Purpose and governance.* Many DC solutions lack a clear retirement objective, beyond their branding or denomination, for instance in terms of replacement rates, and bear too much resemblance to other (shorter-term) investment solutions readily available on the market. The lack of specific retirement purpose is closely linked to governance frictions and the absence of institutional mechanisms to align incentives for originators with long-term investing. Notably, the use of long-term investment targets to benchmark performance is rare. The use of relative benchmarks is commonplace, even though absolute return objectives are more in line with retirement savings. The reform of governance appears more difficult for small providers, given a relative lack of skills and resources.

○ *Liquidity profile.* DC solutions tend to emphasise relatively high liquidity for investors, regarding the frequency and length of redemption windows and the immediacy of execution of redemption orders.[103] High liquidity in this sense is, however, incoherent with long-term investment for retirement. It does not allow long-term assets to be held to maturity, to build and maintain strategic equity stakes or investment in less-liquid asset classes. Redemptions policies need to be well aligned with the liquidity of the underlying, both in the interest of investor protection and financial stability (de Manuel & Lannoo, 2012).[104]

○ *Asset allocation.* A lack of clear retirement purpose and an inadequate liquidity profile towards investors leads to asset allocation mixes skewed towards short-term instruments, with high liquidity and short maturities.

---

[103] Taxation may, however, deter redemptions before retirement, making the actual liquidity profile of DC solutions in some markets far less-liquid.

[104] Pension solutions need to be fairly illiquid until retirement to maximise the potential risk-adjusted return over the long term. The optimal level of liquidity is, however, a matter of balance (section 1.2).

Solutions therefore tend to hold a disproportionate amount of liquid assets, including cash (Impavido et al., 2010). In addition, some solutions pursue inefficient diversification or suffer from home bias – sometimes as a consequence of inefficient government intervention (Oxera, 2007).

○ *Investment practices.* Similarly, investment practices are conditioned by the pursuit of short-term relative performance rather than long-term absolute return objectives. The available evidence indicates that most DC solutions do not consider asset liability management (ALM) practices. They do not distinguish either, within each solution, between return-seeking and liability-hedging portfolios (Amenc et al., 2012).[105] For life-cycle funds there is also evidence of the use of simplistic approaches, such as deterministic glide paths, without explicit consideration of related risks (Amenc et al., 2012).[106] In connection with investment practices, it is apparent that originators do not adequately account for investment costs or factor them into investment decisions. Yet, investment costs can have a considerable impact on net returns, given compounding and long-term investment horizons (AFM, 2011).

○ *Risk management.* Many solutions do not take into account key risks in close relation to their purpose. In particular, many DC solutions ignore risks in connection to the de-accumulation phase, such as annuity conversion risk or longevity risk (Antolín, 2008; Impavido et al., 2010).[107] At portfolio level, the available evidence is that few solutions operate on a basis of risk budgeting or consider the potential benefits and drawbacks of risk hedging and risk insurance (Amenc et al., 2012).[108]

---

[105] While there are no formal liabilities in defined contribution solutions (this being the main difference with defined benefit solutions), future consumption targets or replacement rates can be seen as absolute return objectives and invite the implementation of flexible asset-liability management frameworks.

[106] A more in-depth discussion of life-cycling is provided in section 3.4.

[107] Annuity conversion risk is given by the short-term volatility of conversion rates utilised to transform a stock of money into an income stream, lasting typically until death. Annuity conversion rates are based on the projected long-term curve of interest rates at the time of conversion. Annuity conversion risk also refers to the risk of an accumulated sum in a defined contribution scheme would experience a fall in value, due to short-term volatility, at the time where redemption and conversion into an annuity is mandated by legislation or the pension contract.

[108] Risk hedging and risk insurance present trade-offs since any risk protection afforded (for instance, protection against changes in currency values, interest rates or inflation) typically needs to be weighed against any counterparty exposure generated and the expense incurred in risk hedging and risk insurance transactions.

◦ *Communications.* Communications to holders of DC pension plans tend to be focused on the current market value of the accumulated investments and pay insufficient attention to retirement goals and the action required by beneficiaries to reasonably achieve those (Antolín and Harrison, 2012). The use of current market values in periodic statements to beneficiaries is useful information but can be heavily affected by short-term volatility in markets, which beneficiaries are typically not in a position to understand. Reactions to perceived loss can result in damaging behaviour by the investor, running against his/her own interest, such as stopping retirement savings (Horack et al., 2010). In many market segments, annual statements do not provide information about the progress achieved by the investor in achieving their retirement objectives (a given consumption level or replacement rate) this fails to convey the long-term nature of the solution and heightens the focus on current market values over other crucial aspects such as contribution levels.

◦ *Investor capabilities.* In designing pension solutions, the characteristics and capabilities of the targeted investors are sometimes ignored and frequently misunderstood. Many solutions grant investors a wide margin of choice regarding asset allocation, even when targeting cohorts with low levels of financial expertise and education (Clark et al., 2012). Choice is typically not only given at the time of subscription but also during the life of the investment, even without the requirement to request expert advice first. Most individuals are ill-equipped to make asset allocation decisions and benefit from simpler solutions where allocations are managed independently by the solution originator in accordance with some criteria set ad initium – in relation to the level of risk the individual is able or willing to bear, including as retirement approaches. Non-assisted choice during the life of the investment can result in knee-jerk reactions to short-term price differences. There is evidence that, by being more hands-on with investment options in a retirement solution, investors increase the likelihood of underperforming, as they lack expertise and experience and are affected by biases, such as buying low and selling high (Weber, 2013).

Despite the shortcomings identified above, good examples of solution design are present in the market place. In improving solution design, these solutions are useful benchmarks for industry, policy-makers and investors. In a perfectly efficient market place, supply and demand would gradually converge towards the best solutions. Yet, market frictions make this convergence difficult in practice, without regulatory and supervisory intervention. In addition to the supply and competition dynamics considered in section 3.2, important frictions are also present in the distribution of solutions, such as: i) closed networks – where only solutions originated by the distributor are sold, ii) inducements paid by originators to distributors – which distort the incentives for distributors to look primarily at the quality of solution design; iii) charging structures in advisory services – where they favour complex over simple solutions.[109]

Trade-offs in solution design...

In improving solution design, best practices in the market place and advances in scientific research should guide industry and policy-makers. The subsection above reviewed typical shortcomings in solution design. While there is ample room for improving the design of defined contribution pensions, a perfect and flawless design does not exist, as a number of trade-offs need to be balanced:

○ *Customisation versus cost.* Individuals have different levels of risk aversion, determined both by subjective preferences and objective factors – including their income and wealth, their human capital potential, their health and their ability to pool resources within family structures (Clark et al., 2012). In a world without transaction costs, the optimal pension solution is specific to each individual, in attention to their level of risk aversion. The customisation of solutions to the characteristics of each beneficiary is frequently referred to as *life-styling*.[110] The advantages of life-styling and customisation, in terms of better outcomes for individuals, need to be weighed against their costs however. Higher standardisation leads to lower costs, thanks to economies of scale and scope. More limited choice will inevitably leave some individuals with a retirement solution that is not fully in line with their risk budget and preferences. Yet, thanks to cost savings, such solutions may ultimately yield superior net returns. Uncertainty and information asymmetries make full customisation illusory in practice. But it is both feasible and economical to group individuals in a few cohorts with similar characteristics. It is argued that most individuals would benefit from high standardisation (section 3.1).[111]

---

[109] Distribution is in close connection with solution design as, frequently, underlying products and instruments are accessed by investors indirectly through an account or wrapper, tied to an advisory or sale service. From a practical point of view, the dividing line between distribution and origination can be very thin.

[110] For instance, an individual with an abundant and secure public pension or with a reliable income stream from real estate could afford to run more risk through a complementary funded pension solution, in exchange for potential higher return.

[111] Individuals with higher-risk budgets can typically access quality investment advice and non-standardised investment solutions with ease. Standardised solutions should focus instead on individuals with lower-risk budgets and more limited access to advice.

◦ *Sophistication versus cost.* More sophistication in solution design, investment practices and risk management has the potential to deliver higher and more secure returns. Expertise and sophistication do, however, come at a cost that reduces net returns. Size, in terms of assets under management and number of participants, allows the spreading of fixed costs, making a higher degree of sophistication affordable. A good example is target-date funds; many of which apply deterministic glide-paths (equity allocation decreasing linearly with time) while more sophisticated stochastic modelling is found to reduce risk and increase risk-adjusted performance (Amenc et al., 2012). While the first alternative is simpler and less expensive, the second is more sophisticated and requires a higher degree of expertise and management.

◦ *Access to less-liquid asset classes versus size and cost.* Many pension solutions, in particular defined contribution, do not invest in less-liquid asset classes, as these tend to: i) be incompatible with redemption policies, as advertised to investors, ii) carry high search and entry costs, and iii) require sizeable minimum investments (entry tickets). Scale eases access to less-liquid asset classes, by spreading related costs among a larger number of participants and facilitating diversification within a larger pool of managed assets. Less-liquid assets have longer-term life-cycles and offer higher potential returns (illiquidity premium). Yet, direct investments in these are unlikely to lead to net positive returns, unless undertaken by schemes with sufficient scale.

◦ *Transferability versus long-term investing.* Higher liquidity towards investors (in terms of redemptions) facilitates investor entry, transfers of savings and competition (section 1.2). However, the high liquidity of solution units is inconsistent with long-term investing and the first objective of any pension solution, namely, delivering a given level of income at retirement. In sum, while some liquidity is beneficial to enable healthy competition and efficient transfers (the consolidation of dispersed pension pots), it needs to be kept at a level compatible with long-term investing.

As these trade-offs illustrate, no optimal pension solution exists and numerous factors need to be balanced to ensure private pensions fulfil their purpose and do so efficiently. Building a pan-European framework for personal pensions represents a unique opportunity to balance these trade-offs and improve the quality and accessibility of personal pensions in Europe, while creating a single market capable of achieving higher scale economies and net returns. The next section proposes a blueprint for pan-European personal pensions.

3.4 A blueprint for pan-European personal pensions

In 2012, the European Commission requested EIOPA to initiate reflections with the objective of providing the Commission with technical advice to develop an

EU-wide framework for the activities and supervision of personal pension funds.[112] EIOPA formed a task force in 2013, composed of national supervisors, with the objective of delivering final advice to the Commission in 2015. A pan-European framework for personal pension solutions is a unique opportunity to: i) increase the quality of solution design and their accessibility, ii) create a single market capable of delivering better value to investors, and iii) to mobilise latent long-term funding towards long-term investing opportunities. In sum, a well-devised framework has the potential to foster both income adequacy at retirement and economic growth (Group of Thirty, 2013; OECD, 2013a).

The design of a pan-European framework for personal pensions should seek to address both dismal net returns and low coverage, by targeting the underlying failures in market structure and shortcomings in solution design. The potential for realising efficiencies and scale economies in a single market is estimated to be very high (European Commission, 2010a). But the challenge also lies in ensuring that the benefits from these would be passed on to investors. A pan-European framework should therefore give full consideration to market structure, in view of both the characteristics and behaviours of demand, and supply and competition dynamics. It would hence need to ensure transparency, facilitate efficient scale and the optimal bundling of services, within a supportive processing infrastructure (section 3.2).

Regarding solution design, the deficiencies observed in terms of governance, liquidity profile, asset allocation, investment practices, risk management and communications indicate that the scope for improved outcomes for investors is also sizeable (section 3.3). Yet, no perfect solution design exists and several trade-offs need to be balanced, referring to i) the levels of customisation or life-styling, sophistication in life-cycling and access to illiquid assets, versus ii) the costs linked to each of these features and the potential relief afforded by scale within a genuine single market (section 3.3).

Regulation has a role to play both in addressing market structure and guiding solution design. By providing a narrow playing field for competition in default solutions and a pan-European processing infrastructure, regulation can ensure that schemes reach sufficient scale to be cost efficient and capable of accessing less-liquid asset classes. By providing a set of best-practice principles regarding solution design, in order to qualify for certification, regulation and supervision can pave the way for solutions of higher quality for all investors. Policy-makers

---

[112] See European Commission (2012). The work-stream initiated by EIOPA excludes occupational pensions.

do not face this task in a vacuum but can rely on best practices already present in the market place and forerunning academic research (Amenc et al., 2012).

In view of the former, the next subsections propose a possible blueprint for the regulatory and supervisory structure needed to build an EU single market for personal pensions. The framework proposed is composed of: i) principle-based rules concerning solution design for qualifying schemes and the alignment of incentives with long-term investing, ii) flexible product rules governing the construction of the default option or options, iii) an accompanying industrial policy and processing architecture and ii) measures addressing communication and distribution. Table 10, at the end of this section, summarises the contents of the proposal in six building blocks.

Principle-based rules to align solution design and incentives...

It is proposed that qualifying solutions – which would be granted a passport for cross-border marketing and distribution to retail investors – should comply with a set of principle-based rules aimed at ensuring the high quality of solution design and a clear retirement purpose. Among others, these principles should include:

- *Having a long-term absolute return target, ideally framed as a replacement rate, or recurring income at retirement – where the benefits afforded by other sources of retirement income are known.*
- *Offering a liquidity profile towards investors (redemption policy) coherent with the purpose of saving for retirement and compatible with long-term investing.*
- *Giving explicit consideration to investment horizons, asset-liability management practices (where appropriate), strategic equity stakes and less-liquid asset classes.*
- *Balancing life-styling and life-cycling features, while considering the impact of customisation and sophistication on costs and net returns.*
- *Conducting appropriate risk management practices, while weighing up the benefits and drawbacks of risk hedging and risk insurance.*
- *Giving full consideration to the de-accumulation phase, assisting individuals in making the best choice for de-accumulation and minimising related risks in case of planned annuity conversion.*
- *Catering consciously to the level of expertise and behavioural patterns of the investor cohort targeted, so as to avoid requiring ill-equipped individuals to take periodic investment decisions.*
- *Limiting, to the extent possible, the need for advisory services, for those investor cohorts for whom the fees for such services may significantly erode net returns.*

Principles regarding solution design should be appended by similar conduct of business rules for providers and intermediaries, including:

- *Aligning remuneration practices in line with the retirement objectives of clients and long-term investing.*
- *Conducting full cost accounting and giving careful consideration to investment costs and their impact, given compounding.*
- *Privileging scale, pooling and pan-European solutions over the fast proliferation of products, so as to achieve better value for investors.*

In the proposed framework, the principle-based rules for qualifying schemes presented above would be accompanied by flexible product rules governing solution design, asset allocation and investment practices for default solutions.

Product rules for the default options...

Default options are useful to overcome investor inaction and facilitate choice by investors, while serving as a benchmark against which alternative solutions can be compared. Hence, defaults also play a broader role, as cornerstones of market structure and competition dynamics. Designed to be adequate for most individuals, it is proposed that default options would be sold on an execution-only basis; that is, without the need for investment advice,[113] whose cost can significantly erode net returns over time. It is in this sense (options available on an execution-only basis) that the term *default option* is utilised in this section.

Regarding the design of default solutions, best industry practice and academic research converge towards two main alternatives (Viceira, 2010):

- *Life-style solutions,* customised to the risk budget of each cohort of investors (risk-based investing). *Balanced funds,* where they exploit the advantages of long-term horizons in retirement planning – via strategic equity allocations, investments in fixed income instruments with long maturities and holdings of less-liquid asset classes – are probably the most representative example of life-style retirement solutions. Balanced funds are based on diversification across asset classes but do not incorporate life-cycling.
- *Life-cycle solutions,* which adjust asset allocation towards less risky assets as the individual approaches retirement (age-based investing). These are *target-date funds,* embedding a glide-path whereby allocation to equity and equity-like instruments decreases with age, as the individual exhausts its potential to monetise their human capital. Target-date funds are primarily based on diversification across time and, only secondarily, across asset classes. As the individual approaches retirement, allocations to fixed-

---

[113] The potential to set up a regulated form of simplified advice restricted to default solutions should be explored (FSA, 2011; Thoresen, 2008).

income instruments increase, based on the assumption that bonds are less risky than equities.

Each category of solutions has a number of advantages and drawbacks, which need to be considered in close connection to the de-accumulation phase. Target-date funds can help reduce annuity conversion risk, where such is the chosen pay-out option. By using fixed-income instruments to keep portfolio volatility under control, as retirement approaches they can help to protect the value of accumulated savings from ill-timed and severe falls in markets prices. Asset-liability management practices can be useful in this respect, even though no formal liabilities exist. Solution design and legislation nevertheless need to provide some flexibility regarding the timing for conversion into annuities, as a short-term drop in conversion rates can be very detrimental to beneficiaries.

Balanced funds appear as a better alternative where a draw-down plan is the chosen pay-out option (Antolín et al., 2010). As life expectancy increases draw-down plans may be more beneficial to investors, as they can continue to invest part of their capital during the many years in retirement. A draw-down plan may be combined with the purchase of a deferred annuity to cover longevity risk after a certain age has been reached. The market for annuities, as any other insurance market, should in any event be protected from adverse selection.

Target-date funds and balanced funds are available in the market place but are not homogenous. Some are more sophisticated and better able to handle risk than others. For instance, many target-date funds follow deterministic glide paths, with linearly decreasing allocations to equities, which are automatic and cannot be revised based on market conditions and the relative expensiveness of assets (Amenc et al., 2012). Similarly, not all balanced funds have a clear retirement purpose or conduct appropriate risk management. It is therefore important to identify best practices within these solutions categories.

In identifying best practices, the trade-offs considered in section 3.3 also need to be considered. Higher sophistication and customisation entail costs and lessen the potential for scale economies, as they reduce the ability to pool investments together. As a result, they may lead to similar or lower net returns than simpler and more standardised solutions. The EU single market represents, however, a significant opportunity to raise the level of sophistication and competition, without reducing net returns for investors, as efficient scale can be more easily reached within a bigger market.

In sum, policy-makers can choose to establish a model of either balanced funds or target-date funds as default options. Or alternatively, they could allow both solution categories to be sold on an execution-only basis and leave the choice to individuals, with the support of publicly provisioned information. In deciding which solution category should be regarded as default, system-wide considerations also merit attention, including the transferability of savings and the potential to quickly reach efficient scale, cost-efficiency and enough size to invest in less-liquid asset classes – as these would deliver better value to investors. These considerations support fewer choice and higher standardisation.

Once the choice of the model for default solutions is made, it is proposed that product rules are enacted to ensure the quality of these solutions, in line with best practices. Such product rules should be well defined in order to provide clarity for investors and a level playing field for intermediaries, but flexible enough to allow originators to adapt to changing market circumstances. The adequacy of the rules would be periodically monitored by an EU supervisor (EIOPA) with powers to introduce or propose changes as needed. Product rules for default options would address areas such as:

- *Portfolio construction, eligible assets and permissible investment practices.*
- *The liquidity profile of product units (redemption policies for investors).*
- *Risk management function and practices.*
- *Retirement objectives, connection with the de-accumulation phase and information to participants.*

Accompanying industrial policy and infrastructure...

The characteristics of demand and supply in the market for personal pensions, as considered in section 3.2 tend to promote product proliferation and branding over solution quality and cost-efficiency. While introducing product rules for a default solution can indeed help in raising solution quality overall, also in the non-default space, industrial policy measures are needed to facilitate scale and minimise administration costs, while fostering healthy competition based on quality rather than marketing.

It is argued that an EU single market for personal pensions may not deliver full value to investors unless it is accompanied by a pan-European processing infrastructure for qualifying solutions, following the successful model of the Swedish Premium Pension System (section 3.2). The existence of a single clearing house and blind accounts would minimise administration costs, while facilitating comparability and switching across providers from everywhere in Europe. It would also allow for the establishment of genuinely pan-European products, simultaneously available for retail clients in all member states under equal pricing, in contrast to the situation observed in market segments such as UCITS, at the forefront of European integration today.

The use of blind accounts would result in a reduction in marketing costs, and help focus competition on quality. End investors would not be communicated to providers, who would have as their only client a central agency with greater bargaining power. Following the Swedish model, this agency would be able to seek rebates in management fees, as asset under management would grow, redistributing the benefits of scale economies towards beneficiaries.

In addition, in the default solution space, product rules should be accompanied by a narrow playing field for competition among providers. It is proposed that each provider (whether insurer, asset manager or other intermediary) would only be allowed to offer *one* product per default solution category recognised by regulation. For instance, if balanced fund products are the chosen default, each provider would only be able to sell one of such funds.

Targeted communications and tailored distribution...

Communications with beneficiaries play an important role in the alignment of incentives of providers. As considered in section 3.3 (above), communications in DC pensions sometimes focus excessively on current market values over other important aspects – notably, whether the investor is on track to meet his/her goals. Where they solely emphasise current market values, affected by short-term volatility, communications fail to convey the long-term nature of pension solutions and can lead to knee-jerk reactions by investors.

A pan-European framework for personal pension solutions would need to be complemented with rules governing the content and format of pre-contractual and ongoing (periodic) communications with beneficiaries. For pre-contractual disclosure, the key information document (KID) standard, proposed under the packaged retail investment products (PRIPs) initiative, is undoubtedly a step forward in easing understanding and comparison by beneficiaries, before they decide on their purchase. It is important that the KID standard is well adapted to the characteristics of investing under a long-term horizon with a retirement purpose – and should be aligned with the future EU framework for personal pension solutions.[114]

As regards ongoing disclosure, regulatory intervention is needed to ensure that periodic communications with beneficiaries follow best practices and are very similar across intermediaries, at least for default solutions. Market best practice and academia converge towards de-emphasising market values and providing actionable information to investors (NAPF, 2012; Antolín & Harrison, 2012). The format and content of communications also need to factor in the cognitive and behavioural limitations of individuals (EIOPA, 2013a).[115]

Defined contribution pensions have been frequently utilised to minimise the volatility of consumption (funding) during accumulation, ignoring the likely

---

[114] See legislative proposal COM (2012) 352 final.

[115] For a more in-depth discussion of disclosure practices and investor protection see section 2.3 in this report.

outcomes at retirement or leaving them as an afterthought, poorly explained to investors. As a result, contributions to DC pensions are much lower than in DB schemes (section 3.1). Communication has an important role to play in reversing this perverse trend, empowering individuals to take action. Annual statements should therefore present easy-to-understand projections of the level of income that can be expected upon retirement and inform beneficiaries as to whether they are on track to meet their targets or need to contribute more.[116]

In addition to communications, it is proposed that the future EU framework for personal pensions would be accompanied by specific distribution rules. In effect, distribution is the cornerstone of a successful market structure, capable of delivering value to investors. Distribution rules should distinguish between default and non-default solutions:

○ *Default solutions* would be sold on an execution-only basis, that is, without the requirement to receive investment advice or other forms of sale services. The availability of default solutions on an execution-only basis is judged to be an essential element of the proposed framework, as it would both foster access and scale – coupled with the other measures proposed, notably, a single clearing house and one product per intermediary. To ensure full understanding and eased choice, it is proposed that a single pan-European online information point would be established for default options. On this site, individuals would find both generic information about each solution category and a comparison of all products available on the market under each default category (if more than one category).[117] The potential to set up a regulated form of simplified advice restricted to default solutions should be explored (FSA, 2011; Thoresen, 2008).

○ *Non-default solutions* would require investment advice to be purchased. Yet, it is proposed that special suitability requirements would apply, including broad market coverage and explicit consideration of the cumulative impact of costs and fees (section 2.3).

Table 10 summarises this section by presenting the six building blocks of the proposed pan-European framework for personal pensions: i) principle-based regulation of solution design, ii) product regulation for default options, iii) conduct of business rules for solution providers, iv) a single pan-European

---

[116] Projections should, however, avoid giving any misrepresentation in relation to the lack of any formal guarantee. In addition to the content of periodic disclosure formats themselves, investor education, generic information and non-commercial advice are also important to avoid misrepresentation in this respect. Projections are based on numerous assumptions and are more uncertain the longer the time remaining before retirement.

[117] Originators would contribute to the cost and maintenance of this online service.

processing infrastructure, v) communications with actionable information for investors, and vi) a supportive distribution framework, separate for default and other qualifying solutions.

Table 10. Building blocks for a pan-European framework on personal pensions

SOLUTION DESIGN

- Principle-based regulation of solution design for non-default option(s)
- Explicit consideration of retirement purpose and long-term horizon
- Long-term absolute-return objectives in terms of replacement rates
- Consideration of de-accumulation phase (annuities, draw-downs)

DEFAULT OPTION(S)

- Product regulation of default option (or a limited number of options)
- Life-cycling and life-styling features or options (limited or no range)
- Eligible assets and permissible investment practices
- Allocation range per asset class, including less-liquid asset classes

SOLUTION PROVIDERS

- Resources and expertise
- Alignment of incentives with long-term investment horizon
- Conflicts of interest in asset management value chain
- Industrial organisation and market structure policy (size, access to less-liquid asset classes, cost)

INFRASTRUCTURE

- Pan-European processing architecture
- Pan-European clearing house for default options
- Administration of contributions
- Unbundling of services with lower efficient scale
- Uniform regulation of holding rights and transfers

COMMUNICATION

- Full fee transparency, based on harmonised and simple fee structures
- Standardised pre-contractual disclosure, supported by a single pan-European online information point
- Annual statements focused on replacement rates and follow-up actions by members

DISTRIBUTION

- Special suitability requirements, with broad market coverage and explicit consideration of the cumulative impact of costs and fees
- Professional standards for sales staff
- Execution-only access for default option(s) supported by publicly-provisioned information

Source: Author.

By way of practical examples, Boxes 9 and 10 respectively present a concept delivery framework and a concept default solution for pan-European personal pensions. These two concepts were presented by the representatives from EFAMA and Nordea during the Task Force meetings and are broadly reproduced here for illustration purposes.

Box 9. The example of the ´OCERP´ framework for personal pension products

The Task Force discussions benefited from the presentation of a concept framework to organise the delivery of European pension solutions, under the acronym ´OCERP´ (officially certified European retirement plan). This box presents the main points of the presentation delivered to the Task Force by Bernard Delbecque (European Fund and Asset Management Association, EFAMA). The OCERP concept, as presented to the Task Force, would:

- Be based on individual accounts (one account per person) and personal ownership of pension assets.
- Comply with a set of unified standards for a personal pension product to qualify as an OCERP, for the governance and administrative organization of OCERP providers and for the distribution of the OCERP.
- Be offered across Europe once certified by a competent authority in one member state, upon notice to the authorities of another member state.
- Be offered by insurers, banks, asset managers and pension funds, as long as they comply with the regulatory framework for OCERPs and OCERP providers.
- Restrict the range of investment options from which members can choose according to their different risk-return profiles.
- Put in place mechanisms to help individuals make well-informed choices, notably by presenting the risk-reward profile of the investment options, standard pre-enrolment information and full transparency of costs.
- Offer a default investment option to help individuals who may be unwilling to make a choice.
- Offer a range of solutions for the payout phase, including annuities, lump-sums, phased draw-down plans or combined solutions.

Full details about the OCERP proposal can be found in EFAMA (2010) and EFAMA (2013), referenced in the bibliography of this report.

Box 10. The example of ´Simple´ balanced funds

The Task Force discussions benefited from the presentation of a concept pension solution, branded ´Simple´ and an accompanying market structure. This box reproduces the main points of the presentation delivered by Ole Stæhr (Nordea Wealth Management) to the Task Force. This ´Simple´ concept, as presented to the Task Force, would involve:

An investment vehicle rather than a wrapper...

- ○ 'Simple' products would be investment vehicles, which retail investors would be able to directly access as an alternative to UCITS, AIFs and securities.
- ○ 'Simple' could be part of a wrapper (for instance, the OCERP, an insurance policy or a defined-contribution scheme providing insurance cover for disability, death and longevity and different pay out models). It should also be possible to purchase the investment vehicle separately.

A pan-European investment vehicle...

- ○ Regulated by EU legislation, it could be based on the proposed ELTIF framework for faster adoption and easier implementation.
- ○ National supervisors would authorise and award the 'Simple' status to qualifying products.
- ○ Certified 'Simple' products would receive a European passport with immediate effects for cross-border selling in all EU member states simultaneously.
- ○ Originators would hold 0.25% of assets under management in capital and at least €5m.
- ○ Every 'Simple' product would be denominated in EUR currency to ensure comparability.

Designed for the accumulation phase...

- ○ 'Simple' products would allow retail investors to accumulate and invest their savings.
- ○ The de-accumulation would be best managed by other products (annuities, draw-down plans...)
- ○ As the objective would be to store wealth, no dividends would be paid out.

Set as the default investment solution...

- ○ To maximise the economies of scale and the derived cost-effectiveness.
- ○ To facilitate investment decisions and steer asset allocation in line with investment horizons, helping investors to overcome myopic risk aversion.

Limited to one 'Simple' per product originator...

- ○ To limit choice and foster competition, increasing the value for investors, as a result of commoditisation.

- Originators would label the product 'Simple' + brand name (for instance, 'Simple' Nordea)

With full transparency and easy comparability...

- A single homepage (such as www.simple.org) would hold information in all EU-27 languages about the product concept and all 'Simple' products available in the EU market.
- Standardised disclosure and product information.
- Product providers would pay an annual fee for administering the product concept and website.

Asset allocation in line with long-term investment horizon...

- EU guidelines (issued by the EU supervisor) would set asset allocation targets and permissible ranges.
- Moderate allocation to alternative asset classes, including infrastructure, venture capital, non-listed equities, real estate or high-quality securitisation.

Asset sector	Target allocation (%)	Asset class	Target allocation (%)	Allocation range (%)
Stocks	30	European equities	10	20-40
		Global equities	20	45-70
Bonds	60	European Investment grade	40	45-70
		Global investment grade	15	
		Global High Yield	5	0-10
Alternatives	10	Private equity / venture capital	2.5	0-5
		Real Estate	5	0-10
		EU infrastructure	2.5	0-5

- Benchmarking would be discouraged; instead the goal would be to maximise returns within the guidelines (allocation ranges).
- The use of investment hedging instruments would be out of scope (except currency derivatives against euro since the funds would be euro denominated).

Incorporating sustainability criteria...

- Voting shareholder proxies would be in accordance with environmental, social and governance (ESG) criteria.
- Commitment to engagement with management on issues such as ESG disclosure, executive compensation, worker safety, climate change and others.
- Initiating or supporting shareholder resolutions at annual stockholders meetings aimed at persuading companies to adopt higher standards of responsibility.
- Supporting public policy initiatives that promote greater corporate sustainability, transparency and accountability.

Easily transferable...

- It is suggested that redemption should be possible quarterly but be claimed at least 14 days before the end of each quarter.
- Payments would be made electronically only.

And built upon efficient pan-European administration...

- Within a freely competitive single market, driven by completion on both costs and investment performance.
- The platform for 'Simple' should include a central clearing house that would route subscriptions and redemptions to the preferred 'Simple' originator.
- 'Simple' originators would have the responsibility of investing and providing information to the clearing house.
- Individual taxation would need to be handled locally by the providers of wrappers that would incorporate a 'Simple' product as underlying investment similar to UCITS funds, securities and others. The wrapper would utilise the existing contribution-collection infrastructure in the local market.

* * * *

*

REFERENCES

AFM (Netherlands Authority for the Financial Markets) (2011), "Kosten pensioenfondsen verdienen meer aandacht", (The costs of pension funds deserve more attention), AFM investigation report, Amsterdam.

Amenc, N. and S. Sender (2010), "Are Hedge-Fund UCITS the Cure-All?", EDHEC Risk Institute, Nice.

Amenc, N., F. Cocquemas, L. Martellini and S. Sender (2012), "Response to the European Commission White Paper an Agenda for Adequate, Safe and Sustainable Pensions", EDHEC Risk Institute, Nice.

Amenc, N., L. Martellini and S. Sender (2009), "Impact of Regulations on the ALM of European Pension Funds", EDHEC Risk Institute, Nice, January.

Ang, A. and K.N. Kjaer (2011), "Investing for the Long Run", Netspar Discussion Paper No. 11/2011-104, Netspar (Network for Studies on Pensions, Aging and Retirement), Tilburg.

Antolín, P. (2008), "Policy Options for the Payout Phase", OECD Working Papers on Insurance and Private Pensions, No. 25, OECD, Paris.

Antolín, P. and D. Harrison (2012), Annual DC Pension Statements and the Communications Challenge, OECD Working Papers on Finance, Insurance and Private Pensions, No. 19, OECD, Paris.

Antolín, P., S. Payet and J. Yermo (2010), "Assessing Default Investment Strategies in Defined Contribution Pension Plans", *Financial Market Trends*, Vol. 2010, No. 1.

Bank for International Settlements (2011), "Fixed income strategies of insurance companies and pension funds", Committee on the Global Financial System (CGFS), CGFS Papers No. 44, BIS, Basel.

Bannier, C.E., F. Fecht and M. Tyrell (2007), Open-end real estate funds in Germany – genesis and crisis. Deutsche Bundesbank Discussion Paper Series 2: Banking and Financial Studies, No.04, Frankfurt am Main.

Beetsma, R., W.E. Romp and S. Vos (2011), "Voluntary participation and intergenerational risk sharing in a funded pension system", Discussion Paper No. 8312, Centre for Economic Policy Research (CEPR), London.

Bernardino, G. (2012), *Letter to Commissioner Barnier regarding the Solvency II timetable*, European Insurance and Occupational Pensions Authority (EIOPA), Frankfurt am Main, 4 October.

BlackRock (2012), Balancing Risk, Return and Capital Requirements: The Effect of Solvency II on Asset Allocation and Investment Strategy, Economist Intelligence Unit, London.

BME Consulting (2007), "The EU Market for Consumer Long-term Retail Saving Vehicles", The BME Group, Madrid.

Célérier, C. and B. Vallée (2012), "What Drives Financial Innovation? A Look into the European Retail Structured Products Market", HEC Working Paper, Hautes études commerciales de Paris.

Charter, N., S. Huck and R. Inderst (2010), "Consumer Decision-Making in Retail Investment Services: A Behavioural Economics Perspective", European Commission, November.

Chetty, R., J.N. Friedman, S. Leth-Petersen, T. Nielsen and T. Olsen (2012), "Active vs. Passive Decisions and Crowd-out in Retirement Savings Accounts: Evidence from Denmark", NBER Working Paper No. 18565, National Bureau of Economic Research, Cambridge, MA, November.

Chew, T., M. Kluettgens and C. Murray (2013), "EIOPA Long Term Guarantee Assessment (LTGA) - Scope, Methodology and Application", Towers Watson, New York, NY, January.

Christian, G. (2008), "Intergenerational risk-sharing and risk-taking of a pension fund", *Journal of Public Economics*, Elsevier, Vol. 92(5-6), pp. 1463-1485, June.

Clark, G., K. Strauss and J. Knox-Hayes (2012), *Saving for Retirement*, Oxford: Oxford University Press.

Cocquemas, F. (2013), "Towards Better Consideration of Pension Liabilities in European Union Countries", EDHEC Risk Institute, Nice.

De Larosière et al. (2009), "Report of the High-Level Group on Financial Supervision in the EU", European Commission, Brussels.

De Meza, D., B. Irlenbusch and D. Reyniers (2008), "Financial Capability: A Behavioural Economics Perspective", Consumer Research Paper No. 69, Financial Services Authority (FSA), London.

Della Croce, R. (2011), "Pension Funds Investment in Infrastructure", OECD Working Papers on Finance, Insurance and Private Pensions, No. 13, Paris.

de Manuel Aramendía, M. (2012), "Will the PRIPs' KID live up to its promise to protect investors?", ECMI Commentary No. 33 / July, Centre for European Policy Studies (CEPS) and European Capital Markets Institute (ECMI), Brussels.

de Manuel Aramendía, M. and K. Lannoo (2012), *Rethinking Asset Management: From Financial Stability to Investor Protection and Economic Growth*, CEPS-ECMI Task Force Report, Centre for European Policy Studies (CEPS) and European Capital Markets Institute (ECMI), Brussels.

de Manuel Aramendía, M. and D. Valiante (2013), "A life-cycle approach to investor protection", ECMI Policy Brief (forthcoming), Centre for European Policy Studies (CEPS) and European Capital Markets Institute (ECMI), Brussels.

EFAMA (2010), "Revisiting the landscape of European long-term savings – A call for action from the asset management industry", European Fund and Asset Management Association, Brussels.

_____ (2011), "Asset Management in Europe", European Fund and Asset Management Association, Brussels.

_____ (2012), "What can the industry do to encourage long-term savings?", European Fund and Asset Management Association, Brussels.

_____ (2013), "The OCERP: A Proposal for a European Personal Pension Product", European Fund and Asset Management Association, Brussels, September.

Eichhorst, W., M. Gerard, M.J. Kendzia, C. Mayrhuber, C. Nielsen, G. Rünstler and T. Url (2011), "Pension systems in the EU", Study Commissioned by the European Parliament Committee on Economic and Monetary Affairs, Brussels.

EIOPA (2010), "Cross-border activity of IORPs: Practical issues paper", CEIOPS-DOC-97-10, Committee of European Insurance and Occupational Pensions Supervisors, Frankfurt am Main.

_____ (2011), "Report on the fifth Quantitative Impact Study (QIS5) for Solvency II", European Insurance and Occupational Pensions Authority, Frankfurt am Main.

_____ (2012a), "Report on market developments – IORPs", European Insurance and Occupational Pensions Authority, Frankfurt am Main.

_____ (2012b), "Statistical Annex to the Financial Stability Report 2012 (second half-year report)", European Insurance and Occupational Pensions Authority, Frankfurt am Main.

_____ (2012c), "Financial Stability Report 2012 (second half-year report)", European Insurance and Occupational Pensions Authority, Frankfurt am Main.

_____ (2012d), "Opinion on interim measures regarding Solvency II", European Insurance and Occupational Pensions Authority, Frankfurt am Main.

_____ (2012e), "Advice to the European Commission on the review of the IORP Directive 2003/41/EC", European Insurance and Occupational Pensions Authority, Frankfurt am Main.

_____ (2013a), "Opinion on Supervisory Response to a Prolonged Low Interest Rate Environment", European Insurance and Occupational Pensions Authority, Frankfurt am Main.

_____ (2013b), "Report on QIS on IORPs", European Insurance and Occupational Pensions Authority, Frankfurt am Main, July.

_____ (2013c), "Cover note for the Consultation on Guidelines on preparing for Solvency II", European Insurance and Occupational Pensions Authority, Frankfurt am Main.

_____ (2013d), "Long-Term Guarantees Assessment - Launch information for participants", European Insurance and Occupational Pensions Authority, Frankfurt am Main.

_____ (2013e), "Discussion Paper on Standard Formula Design and Calibration for Certain Long Term Investments", European Insurance and Occupational Pensions Authority, Frankfurt am Main.

_____ (2013f), "Good practices on information provision for DC schemes - Enabling occupational DC scheme members to plan for retirement", European Insurance and Occupational Pensions Authority, Frankfurt am Main, January.

_____ (2013g), "Technical Findings on the Long-Term Guarantees Assessment", European Insurance and Occupational Pensions Authority, Frankfurt am Main.

_____ (2013h), "Discussion Paper on a possible EU-single market for personal pension products", European Insurance and Occupational Pensions Authority, Frankfurt am Main.

Eurofinuse (2013), "Private Pensions: The Real Return", European Federation of Financial Users, Brussels.

ECB (2013a), "The Eurosystem Household Finance and Consumption Survey - Results from the first wave", ECB Statistics Paper Series, European Central Bank, Frankfurt.

_____ (2013b), Introductory statement to the press conference following the meeting of the Governing Council, 4 April.

European Commission (2008), Explanatory memorandum to the Solvency II amended proposal.

_____ (2009a), Communication on Packaged Retail Investment Products. COM (2009) 204 final.

_____ (2009b), Update on the Commission Work on PRIPS, December.

_____ (2009c), "Impact assessment accompanying the communication from the Commission on packaged retail investment products", European Commission, COM (2009) 204.

_____ (2010a), Green Paper towards adequate, sustainable and safe European pension systems.

_____ (2010b), Europe 2020 Flagship Initiative - Innovation Union.

_____ (2011a), Call for Advice from the European Insurance and Occupational Pension Authority for the Review of Directive 2003/41/EC (IORP II) (p. 12), Brussels.

_____ (2011b), A growth package for integrated European infrastructures.

_____ (2011c), An action plan to improve access to finance for SMEs.

_____ (2012a), White Paper - An Agenda for Adequate, Safe and Sustainable Pensions (p. 40).

_____ (2012b), "Annual Growth Survey 2012".

_____ (2012c), Letter of Jonathan Faull to Gabriel Bernardino on the calibration of capital charges in Solvency II for long-term investing.

_____ (2012d), Towards a real single market for occupational pensions offering greater choice and better protection for pensioners, (March), Press Note 1–6.

_____ (2012e), A stronger European Industry for Growth and Economic Recovery.

_____ (2012f), Letter of Jonathan Faull to Gabriel Bernardino on the Long-Term Guarantee Assessment.

_____ (2012g), Consultation document on UCITS, product rules, liquidity management, depositary, money market funds and long-term investments.

_____ (2012h), Single Market Act II - Together for New Growth. COM (2012) 573 final.

_____ (2012i), Request for technical advice to develop an EU Single Market for personal pension schemes.

_____ (2013a), Green Paper on the long-term financing of the European economy.

_____ (2013b), Impact Assessment Accompanying the Green Paper on the long-term financing of the European economy.

_____ (2013c), Occupational Pension Funds (IORP): Next Steps.

_____ (2013d), Impact Assessment Accompanying the Proposal for a Regulation on European Long-term Investment Funds (ELTIFs). SWD (2013) 230 final.

_____ (2013e), Towards social investment for growth and cohesion.

EVCA (2012), "Calibration of Risk and Correlation in Private Equity", European Private Equity and Venture Capital Association, Brussels.

Financial Services Authority (FSA) (2009), "Using the FSA's pension-switching advice suitability assessment template", London.

_____ (2011), "Guidance consultation on a process of simplified advice".

Financial Stability Board (FSB) (2013), "Financial regulatory factors affecting the availability of long-term investment finance", Basel, February.

GfK (2011), "Monitoring consumer markets in the European Union".

Giesecke, K., F.A. Longstaff, S. Schaefer and I. Strebulaev (2010), "Corporate Bond Default Risk: A 150-year Perspective", NBER Working Paper Series, No. 15848, National Bureau of Economic Research, Cambridge, MA.

Group of Thirty (G30) (2013), "Long-term Finance and Economic Growth", Working Group on Long-term Finance, Washington, D.C.

Gründl, H. (2013), "Impact of prudential rules on asset allocation", presentation delivered at the fourth meeting of the CEPS ECMI Task Force on Long-term Investing and Retirement Savings, Centre for European Policy Studies (CEPS) and European Capital Markets Institute (ECMI), 14 March, Brussels.

Guardiancich, I. (2010), "Sweden - Current pension system: First assessment of reform outcomes and output", European Social Observatory, Brussels.

Haupt, M. and S. Kluth (2013), "Take a chance on me - Can the Swedish premium pension serve as a role model for Germany's Riester scheme?", Munich Centre for the Economics of Aging Discussion Paper, Max Planck Institute for Social Law and Social Policy, Munich.

Hernandez, D.G. and F. Stewart (2008), "Comparison of Costs + Fees in Countries with Private Defined Contribution Pension Systems", IOPS Working Paper No. 6, International Organisation of Pension Supervisors (IOPS).

Hirose, K. (ed.) (2002), Pension Reform in Central and Eastern Europe", International Labour Organisation (ILO), Genève.

Hirschman, A.O. (1970), *Exit, Voice, and Loyalty - Responses to Decline in Firms, Organizations, and States*, Cambridge, MA: Harvard University Press.

Hollanders, D. (2010), "The political economy of intergenerational risk sharing", Discussion Paper No. 2010–102, CentER, Tilburg University, Tilburg.

Holzmann, R. (2012), "Global Pension Systems and Their Reform", Institute for the Study of Labor (IZA), Discussion Paper No.6800, Bonn.

Horack, S., E. Imison and A. Terry (2010a), "Understanding reactions to volatility and loss", National Employment Saving Trust (NEST), Peterborough.

Horack, S., E. Imison and A. Terry (2010b), "Understanding reactions to volatility and loss", National Employment Saving Trust, (NEST), Peterborough.

Höring, D. (2012), "Will Solvency II Market Risk Requirements Bite? The Impact of Solvency II on Insurers' Asset Allocation", ICIR Working Paper Series No. 11, International Center for Insurance Regulation, Frankfurt.

IFF Research and YouGov (2009), UCITS Disclosure Testing Research Report, prepared for the European Commission.

IISD (International Institute for Sustainable Development) (2012), "Financial Stability and Systemic Risk: Lenses and Clocks", Winnipeg, Manitoba, Canada.

Impavido, G., E. Lasagabaster and M. Garcia-Huitron (2010), "New Policies for Mandatory Defined Contribution Pensions: Industrial Organization Models and Investment Products", World Bank Publication No. 2462, World Bank, Washington, D.C.

International Monetary Fund (IMF) (2013), "Global Financial Stability Report - Old Risks, New Challenges", Washington, D.C., April.

International Organization of Securities Commissions (IOSCO) (2012), "Suitability Requirements with respect to the Distribution of Complex Financial Products", Consultation Report, Madrid.

_____ (2013), "Suitability Requirements With Respect To the Distribution of Complex Financial Products", Final Report, January, Madrid.

IRI (Institute for Responsible Investment) (2006), *Handbook on Responsible Investment across Asset Classes*, Boston College – Carrol School of Management, Centre for Corporate Citizenship, Boston, MA.

Kay, J. (2012), "The Kay review of UK equity markets and long-term decision making", HM Government, London.

KPMG (2012), "The Solvency II discount rate: Nothing is simple", KPMG.

Manning, M.J. (2004), "Exploring the relationship between credit spreads and default probabilities", Bank of England Working Paper No.225, Market Infrastructure Division, Financial Stability, Bank of England, London

Martellini, L. and V. Milhau (2011), "An Integrated Approach to Asset-Liability Management", EDHEC Risk Institute, Nice, June.

Morgan Stanley (2013), "Releasing the Pressure from Low Yields: Should Insurers Consider Re-risking Investments?", Blue Paper, Morgan Stanley Research, London.

Roxburgh, Ch., S. Lund, R. Dobbs, J. Manyika and H. Wu (2011), "The emerging equity gap: Growth and stability in the new investor landscape", McKinsey Global Institute, December.

NAPF (2012), "Defining Ambition: Views from the industry on achieving risk sharing", NAPF research publication, Cheapside, UK.

OECD (2005), Pensions Glossary, Paris.

_____ (2011a), "Pension funds investment in infrastructure", OECD Survey, Paris.

_____ (2011b), "Promoting Longer-term Investment by Institutional Investors: Selected Issues and Policies", *Financial Market Trends*, No. 1, Paris.

_____ (2011c), "Pension Markets in Focus", Paris, July (8).

_____ (2011d), *Pensions at a Glance 2011: Retirement-income system in OECD and G-20 countries*, Paris.

_____ (2012), "OECD Pensions Outlook 2012", Paris.

_____ (2013a), "Institutional Investors and Long-term Investing", Project Brochure, Paris.

_____ (2013b), "National Accounts at a Glance 2013", Paris.

Observatoire de l'épargne réglementée (OER) (2011), 2011 Rapport Annuel de l'Observatoire de l'Epargne Réglementée, Banque de France, Paris.

Office for National Statistics (UK) (2012), "Occupational Pension Schemes Survey, 2011", ONS Statistical Bulletin.

Oxera (2007), "The effect of cross-border investment restrictions on certain pension schemes in the EU", report prepared for the European Commission, DG Internal Market and Services, Brussels, April.

Prime Collateralised Securities initiative (PCS) (2013), "Europe in transition - Bridging the funding gap", White Paper, London.

Severinson, C. and J. Yermo (2012), "The Effect of Solvency Regulations and Accounting Standards on Long-Term Investing", OECD Working Papers on Finance, Insurance and Private Pensions, No. 30, OECD, Paris.

Standard & Poor's (2013), "Q&A on the Future of Solvency II: Pragmatism is Likely to Prevail", London.

Strategic Insight (2011), "Fund Fees in Europe: Analysing Investment Management Fees, Distribution Fees and Operating Expenses", report prepared for European Fund and Asset Management Association (EFAMA), October.

Tapia, W. and J. Yermo (2008), "Fees in Individual Account Pension Systems", OECD Working Papers on Insurance and Private Pensions, No. 27, OECD, Paris.

Thoresen, O. (2008), "Thoresen Review of generic financial advice: final report", HM Treasury, London.

Towers Watson (2012), "Solvency II - The matching adjustment and implications for long-term savings", New York, NY.

Turner, A. (2009), "The Turner Review - A regulatory response to the global banking crisis", Financial Services Authority (FSA), London.

Valiante, D. and K. Lannoo (2011), *MiFID 2.0: Casting New Light on Europe's Capital Markets*, CEPS-ECMI Task Force Report, Centre for European Policy Studies (CEPS) and European Capital Markets Institute (ECMI), Brussels.

Viceira, L. (2010), "Application of Advances in Financial Theory and Evidence to Pension Fund Design in Developing Economies", in Hinz,R., R. Heinz, P. Antolin and J. Yermo (eds), *Evaluating the Financial Performance of Pension Funds*, chapter 7, World Bank, Washington, D.C.

Weaver, K. (2005), "Social Security Smörgåsbord? Lessons from Sweden's Individual Pension Accounts", Policy Brief No. 140, Brookings Institution, Washington, D.C.

Webber, L. and R. Churm (2007), "Decomposing corporate bond spreads", Bank of England Quarterly Bulletin Q4, BoE, London, pp. 533–541.

Weber, S.M. (2013), "Most Vanguard IRA investors shot par by staying the course: 2008-2012", Vanguard research paper, The Vanguard Group, Inc, Valley Forge, PA.

Wood, A., D. Wintersgill and N. Baker (2012), "Pension landscape and charging: Quantitative and qualitative research with employers and pension providers", DWP Research Report No. 804, Department for Work and Pensions (DWP), London.

Impavido, G., E. Lasagabaster and M. García-Huitrón (2010), "New Policies for Mandatory Defined Contribution Pensions - Industrial Organisation Models and Investment Products", World Bank Publication No. 2462, World Bank, Washington, D.C.

World Economic Forum and Oliver Wyman (2011), "The Future of Long-term Investing", World Economic Forum, Geneva.

ANNEXES

Annex 1. Additional Tables

Table A.1: Evolution of household financial holdings 2000-2010, extended table*

	Currency and deposits		Securities other than shares		Shares and other equity		Insurance technical reserves		Other holdings	
	2000	2010	2000	2010	2000	2010	2000	2010	2000	2010
Austria	51%	47%	7%	9%	24%	22%	18%	20%	1%	2%
Belgium	21%	32%	19%	9%	44%	31%	13%	26%	3%	1%
Czech Rep.	51%	56%	0%	1%	39%	25%	7%	14%	2%	4%
Denmark	21%	19%	8%	4%	23%	29%	46%	47%	2%	1%
Estonia	34%	21%	0%	0%	55%	69%	1%	6%	10%	4%
Finland	33%	35%	1%	3%	44%	40%	19%	19%	3%	2%
France	32%	29%	3%	2%	32%	24%	28%	37%	5%	8%
Germany	35%	40%	6%	5%	28%	19%	29%	35%	1%	1%
Greece	44%	77%	8%	8%	43%	9%	2%	4%	2%	2%
Hungary	42%	34%	9%	6%	34%	36%	10%	21%	6%	4%
Italy	23%	30%	17%	19%	46%	30%	11%	18%	3%	3%
Netherlands	17%	23%	3%	2%	26%	13%	52%	61%	2%	1%
Poland	60%	43%	1%	1%	22%	27%	7%	27%	10%	3%
Portugal	36%	37%	4%	6%	32%	27%	12%	19%	15%	10%
Slovak Rep.	78%	65%	3%	2%	6%	8%	1%	21%	12%	5%
Spain	40%	49%	3%	3%	40%	29%	14%	15%	3%	4%
Sweden	15%	18%	3%	2%	41%	40%	40%	39%	1%	2%
United King.	21%	28%	1%	1%	23%	15%	52%	52%	3%	3%
Norway	33%	32%	1%	0%	18%	13%	37%	40%	11%	15%
Switzerland	23%	30%	9%	7%	27%	20%	41%	42%	0%	0%
Europe	35%	37%	5%	4%	32%	26%	22%	28%	5%	4%
Canada	19%	23%	5%	2%	34%	35%	36%	36%	6%	4%
Japan	54%	54%	4%	3%	11%	11%	27%	28%	4%	4%
United States	10%	14%	7%	11%	50%	43%	31%	30%	2%	2%

*Data from national accounts. Europe includes listed countries. See also Figure 6 in Chapter 1.
Source: OECD (2013b).

Table A.2: Stylised illustration of the cumulative impact of costs on net returns*

Assumed yearly rate of return	3%	3%	3%	3%	3%	3%	3%
Yearly charge on accumulated value	0.00%	0.15%	0.25%	0.50%	0.75%	1.00%	2.00%
Difference in yearly charge	-	0.15%	0.10%	0.25%	0.25%	1.00%	1.00%

Year t	Yearly contributions	Accumulated contributions	Value year t	Value year t	Value year t	Value year t	Value year t	Value year t	Value year t
10	10,000	100,000	118,077.96	117,065.38	116,395.52	114,738.86	113,107.58	111,501.29	105,318.57
		Total costs at end year 10	0.00	1,012.58	1,682.44	3,339.10	4,970.38	6,576.67	12,759.39
		Total net returns at end year 10	18,077.96	17,065.38	16,395.52	14,738.86	13,107.58	11,501.29	5,318.57
		% Costs over zero-cost case	-	0.86%	1.42%	2.83%	4.21%	5.57%	10.81%
		% Returns over principal invested	-	17.07%	16.40%	14.74%	13.11%	11.50%	5.32%
		Total cost / total net returns	-	5.93%	10.26%	22.66%	37.92%	57.18%	239.90%
20	10,000	200,000	276,764.86	272,047.44	268,954.43	261,399.50	254,091.34	247,021.50	220,966.53
		Total costs at end year 20	0.00	4,717.42	7,810.43	15,365.36	22,673.52	29,743.36	55,798.33
		Total net returns at end year 20	76,764.86	72,047.44	68,954.43	61,399.50	54,091.34	47,021.50	20,966.53
		% Costs over zero-cost case	-	1.70%	2.82%	5.55%	8.19%	10.75%	20.16%
		% Returns over principal invested	-	36.02%	34.48%	30.70%	27.05%	23.51%	10.48%
		Total cost / total net returns	-	6.55%	11.33%	25.03%	41.92%	63.25%	266.13%
30	10,000	300,000	490,026.78	477,227.13	468,912.46	448,862.96	429,821.58	411,734.65	347,956.95
		Total costs at end year 30	0.00	12,799.66	21,114.32	41,163.82	60,205.21	78,292.13	142,069.83
		Total net returns at end year 30	190,026.78	177,227.13	168,912.46	148,862.96	129,821.58	111,734.65	47,956.95
		% Costs over zero-cost case	-	2.61%	4.31%	8.40%	12.29%	15.98%	28.99%
		% Returns over principal invested	-	59.08%	56.30%	49.62%	43.27%	37.24%	15.99%
		Total cost / total net returns	-	7.22%	12.50%	27.65%	46.38%	70.07%	296.24%

* Charge rate applied on the value of accumulated principal and returns at the end of each year. A constant rate of return of 3% per year is assumed.

Source: Author.

Annex 2. Task Force Participants

Chairman

Allan Polack
Chief Executive Officer
Nordea Asset Management

Rapporteurs

Mirzha de Manuel Aramendía
Research Fellow
CEPS - Centre for European Policy Studies
ECMI - European Capital Markets Institute

Karel Lannoo
Chief Executive Officer
CEPS - Centre for European Policy Studies
ECMI - European Capital Markets Institute

Task Force Members

Heiko Beck
Managing Director
Union Asset Management Holding

Patrice Bergé-Vincent
Partner Asset Management Regulatory
PriceWaterhouseCoopers

Pierre Bollon
Director General
AFG - Association Française de la Gestion
    Financière

Ana Breda
Economic Advisor
EFAMA - European Fund and Asset Management
    Association

Lachlan Burn
Partner - Capital Markets
Linklaters

James Burnham
Director
EVCA - European Private Equity and Venture
    Capital Association

Simon Burns
Public Affairs and Research Executive
BVCA - British Private Equity and Venture
    Capital Association

Michael Collins
Public Affairs Director
EVCA - European Private Equity and Venture
    Capital Association

Joanna Cound
Managing Director
Government Affairs and Public Policy
BlackRock

Jean-Baptiste de Franssu
Chairman
Incipit

Nine de Graaf
Trainee Public Affairs
PGGM

Michel de Jonge
Expert Policy Advisor EU Public Affairs
PGGM

Laurent de Smedt
Policy Officer
EVCA - European Private Equity and Venture
    Capital Association

Laure Delahousse
Director of Asset Management and Public Affairs
AFG - Association Française de la Gestion
    Financière

Bernard Delbecque
Director of Economics and Research
EFAMA - European Fund and Asset
    Management Association

Carey Evans
Vice President and Associate Director
Fleishman Hillard

Stephen Fisher
Managing Director
Government Affairs and Public Policy
BlackRock

Jane Gimber
Account Manager Financial Services Practice
Fleishman-Hillard

Julia Hobart
Partner
Oliver Wyman

Christian Hott
Senior Economist
Government and Industry Affairs
Zurich Insurance Company

Fiona Joseph
European Business Manager - Public Policy
Aberdeen Asset Management

Anne Keane
Director
Afore Consulting

Maroussia Klep
Associate
Kreab Gavin Anderson

Agathe Legris
Executive Associate
Kreab Gavin Anderson

Francesca Mollica
Director
Kreab Gavin Anderson

Burkhard Ober
Head of European Affairs Office Brussels
Allianz

Carine Delfrayssi
Deputy Head of International Affairs
AFG - Association Française de la Gestion
    Financière

Claire Fargeot
Head of Standards and Financial Market Integrity
    EMEA
CFA Institute

Martin Gilbert
Chief Executive Officer
Aberdeen Asset Management

Andreas Guth
Public Affairs Manager
INREV - European Association for Investors in
    Non-Listed Real Estate Vehicles

Simon Horner
Deputy Director Strategy
BVCA - British Private Equity and Venture Capital
    Association

Stephane Janin
Director, Head of International Affairs Division
AFG - Association Française de la Gestion
    Financière

Patrik Karlsson
Head of EU Public Affairs, Funds
Prudential

Jesper Kjerside
Partner and Managing Director
BCG - Boston Consulting Group

Kurt Kotzegger
Chief Investment Officer
Equities and Asset Allocation
Raiffeisen Zentralbank Österreich

Andreas Maskow
Attorney-at-Law
Union Asset Management

Anders Nordheim
Head of Research and Policy
Eurosif

Matt Orsagh
Director of Capital Markets Policy
CFA Institute (USA)

Martin Parkes
Director, Government Affairs and Public Policy
BlackRock

Anne Plöger
Regulatory Policy Advisor, European Affairs
   Office
Allianz

Per Bremer Rasmussen
Chief Executive Officer
Danish Insurance Association

Donald Ricketts
Head of Financial Services, Senior Vice President
   and Partner, DirectorFinancial Services
Fleishman-Hillard

Kyoko Sakuma
Senior Research Fellow
Solvay Brussels School of Economics and
   Management

Gordon Scott
Head of EU Policy Development and Public
   Affairs
Prudential

Hannes Sigurdsson
Deputy Director General
Confederation of Icelandic Employers

Ole Leonard Stæhr
Executive Advisor
Nordea Wealth Management

Jaap van Dam
Director Investment Strategy
PGGM

Samantha Walker
Head Public Affairs
Aberdeen Asset Management

Andreas Witzani
Member of the Board
Raiffeisen Zentralbank Österreich

Alastair Woodward
Conducting Officer and Head of Risk
   Luxembourg
Aberdeen Global Services

Paul Pasquali
Head of EU Liaison Office
Raiffeisen Zentralbank

Pablo Portugal
Advocacy
AFME - Finance for Europe

Nickolas Reinhardt
Director
Afore Consulting

Jeff Rupp
Director Public Affairs
INREV - European Association for Investors in
   Non-Listed Real Estate Vehicles

Alexandra Schick
Manager, Legal and Public Affairs
Union Asset Management

Khalid Sheikh
Senior Strategist
PGGM

Cliff Speed
Managing Director
Blackrock Client Solutions

Sandrell Sultana
Associate Director
Kreab Gavin Anderson

Ron van Grinsven
Legal Counsel
PGGM

Rick Watson
Head of Capital Markets
AFME - Finance for Europe

Lara Wolters
Consultant
Afore Consulting

Task Force Observers

Sophie Barbier
Advisor
Caisse des Dépôts

Christophe Bourdillon
Advisor European Public Affairs
Caisse des Dépôts

François Calonne
Director for European and International Affairs
Caisse des Dépôts

Gordon Clark
Director of the Smith School of Enterprise and the
  Environment
University of Oxford

Marc-Antoine Coursaget
Representative European Public Affairs Office
Caisse des Dépôts

Pierre Darbre
Policy Officer
DG Internal Market and Services / Insurance and
  Pensions Unit
European Commission

Olivier Debande
Managerial Adviser, Institutional Strategy
EIB - European Investment Bank

Raffaele Della Croce
Economist, Financial Affairs Division
OECD - Organisation for Economic Co-operation
  and Development

Robin Edme
Senior Advisor Responsible Finance
Office of the Commissioner General for
  Sustainable Development
French Ministry of Ecology and Energy

Andrea Fenech Gonzaga
Lawyer
DG Internal Market and Services / Asset
  Management Unit
European Commission

Mark Fenton-O'Creevy
Professor of Organisational Behaviour
Open University

Christelle Fontbonne-Proniewski
Policy Officer
DG Internal Market and Services / Accounting
  and Financial Reporting
Policy Officer

Julie Galbo
Deputy Director General
Finanstilsynet (Danish Financial Services
  Authority)

Helmut Gründl
Managing Director
ICIR - International Center for Insurance
  Regulation

Cees Karregat
Senior Expert - Pensions
EIOPA - European Insurance and Occupational
  Pensions Authority

Marcin Kawinski
Consumer and Financial Services Expert
Warsaw School of Economics

Barthold Kuipers
Policy Officer - Pensions
EIOPA - European Insurance and Occupational
  Pensions Authority

Jung-Duk Lichtenberger
Policy Officer
DG Internal Market and Services/Insurance and
  Pensions Unit
European Commission

Michael Mainelli
Principal Advisor
Long Finance

Anne-Françoise Mélot
Deputy Head of Unit
DG Internal Market and Services / Accounting
  and Financial Reporting
European Commission

Ian Michael
Manager, Risk and Regulation, Financial
  Services Faculty
ICAEW - Institute of Chartered Accountants in
  England and Wales

Eric Perée
Associate Director, Institutional Affairs
EIB - European Investment Bank

Dawn Robey
Policy Officer
DG Internal Market and Services / Accounting
  and Financial Reporting
European Commission

Timothy Shakesby
Policy Analyst
DG Internal Market and Services / Asset
  Management Unit
European Commission

Diego Valiante
ECMI Head of Research and CEPS Research
  Fellow
ECMI - European Capital Markets Institute
CEPS - Centre for European Policy Studies

Juan Manuel Viver
Policy Officer
EuroFinuse

Esther Wandel
Administrator
DG Internal Market and Services / Asset
  Management Unit
European Commission

Alfredo Panarella
Senior Head of Unit, Institutional Strategy
EIB - European Investment Bank

Guillaume Prache
Managing Director
EuroFinuse

Almoro Rubin de Cervin
Deputy Head of Unit
DG Internal Market and Services / Financial
  Services Policy, Relations with the Council
European Commission

Robert Specterman
Policy Officer
DG Internal Market and Services / Financial
  Services Policy, Relations with the Council
European Commission

Lina Vatenaite
Legal Officer
DG Internal Market and Services / Asset
  Management Unit
European Commission

Tomas Walter
Senior Expert Solvency II
EIOPA - European Insurance and Occupational
  Pensions Authority

Juan Yermo
Deputy Head
Financial Affairs Division
OECD - Organisation for Economic Co-operation
  and Development

Members are individuals who participated in the Task Force. Members may represent a private company, an association, a consumer group, a non-governmental organisation, or any other entity pursuing a commercial or non-commercial interest in the topics discussed. Members contributed to Task Force meetings and provided input to the discussions through presentations and relevant materials for the Final Report. Members contributed to the expenses of the Task Force through a general fee paid by their respective organisation. The findings of the Final Report, independently drafted by CEPS-ECMI Research Fellow, Mirzha de Manuel, do not necessarily reflect the views expressed by Members or their respective organisations (see disclaimer at beginning of Report).

Observers are academics, policy-makers, regulators and supervisors, representing their own views or those of a governmental authority, European institution or other public body. Observers have regularly followed the work of the Task Force, attended one or more meetings, or contributed to the discussion through presentations or other materials.

Rapporteurs are the CEPS-ECMI experts who independently proposed and developed the research programme for the Task Force, conducted all relevant research and drafted the Final Report.

Chair is an internationally recognised expert appointed by CEPS to steer the dialogue during the meetings and ensure that all interests around the table were sufficiently heard. The Chair also advised on the general conduct of the Task Force. The Chair, however, was not involved in the drafting of the Final Report and cannot be identified in any way with its authorship.